Published by hope*books

2217 Matthews Township Pkwy

Suite D302

Matthews, NC 28105

www.hopebooks.com

hope*books is a division of hope*media

Printed in the United States of America

First paperback edition.

Paperback ISBN: 979-8-89185-222-8

Hardcover ISBN: 979-8-89185-199-3

Ebook ISBN: 979-8-89185-223-5

Library of Congress Number: 2025937851

Table of Contents

Foreword

By Hope H. Dover

The empty nest is often talked about as an ending, but rarely as the beginning. For many women, this season arrives with a complex mix of emotions: grief, freedom, uncertainty, and quiet. It's a time when the rhythms that once shaped daily life shift, and with that shift comes the invitation to rediscover who you are and who God is calling you to be now.

That's why this book matters.

Reclaiming Me: Embracing Life and Purpose with an Empty Nest is a collection of stories from women who have walked through this tender transition. Their stories are raw and real, filled with honesty, hope, and the hard-won wisdom that comes from letting go and learning to live differently. They don't pretend this season is easy, but they do show that it can be sacred.

You don't have to be in this chapter of life to be moved by these words. These stories serve as a beautiful reminder that our identity is not found in a role or routine, but in the unshakable truth of who we are in Christ.

Whether you're standing in a quiet home, approaching the threshold of change, or simply learning to trust God with what's next, *Reclaiming Me* invites you to release, rediscover, and reclaim one faithful step at a time.

This isn't the end.

It's a beautiful new beginning.

About the Chapters

Karen Griffith opens the collection by inviting readers to reimagine their homes and lives as sacred spaces of beauty, grace, and order. Drawing from her love of design and a deep longing to nurture, she reflects on what it means to build a home that evolves with us in seasons of transition. With warmth and practical insight, Karen explores how creating a meaningful space can offer comfort, healing, and renewed purpose when the nest begins to empty.

In chapter two, Brenda Woomer shares the quiet revelation that sprouted in an unlikely place. As her sons grew into men and her home grew quiet, Brenda wrestled with what it meant to have purpose beyond parenting. Through vivid storytelling and gentle encouragement, she reminds readers that God still calls us to sow seeds, even when our seasons change, and that the harvest will come.

In "Who Are You: Finding Your Identity in Christ Alone," Jane Harper DeLong shares how she found herself on a new path, one where her worth was no longer tied to motherhood or performance, but to being a child of God. Through her story of rediscovery and renewed faith, Jane offers hope for every woman struggling to answer, "Who am I now?" in the wake of change.

Chapter four challenges the narrative that motherhood ends when children leave the nest. In this empowering chapter, Kathleen A. Giles reframes the role of the empty-nest mom as a "matriarch mama," still deeply influential in the lives of her children and community. With wisdom and humor, Kathleen calls women to embrace their God-given authority and recognize the lasting impact of their faith, presence, and love.

In a quiet season of reflection, Hope Intercedes finds herself asking a question many women face in midlife: "Who am I now?" As responsibilities shift and roles evolve, she learns to listen for God's voice and rediscover her identity rooted not in doing, but in being. With heartfelt honesty and hope, this chapter reminds readers that their worth is unwavering and their story is far from over.

Through the lens of personal loss, deep introspection, and unexpected beauty, Amy Duckworth Harrington paints a picture of grief, freedom, and rediscovery in chapter six. Comparing her journey to that of a seabird taking flight, she explores how the empty nest invites us not only to mourn what was, but also to soar into what can be. Her story is a gentle invitation to embrace both wings and wind.

Francesca Follone-Montgomery reflects on the three years that shaped her spiritual and emotional transformation in her chapter. From the pain of letting go to the peace of sacred surrender, she outlines how growth often comes in unexpected waves. Rooted in faith and grounded in grace, her story offers a pathway for others seeking to cultivate hope and purpose in their own post-parenting journey.

In chapter eight, Michelle Castro-Proud shares how a season of loss and transition brought her to a place of deeper faith. As she welcomed God into the places of her greatest need, she discovered healing, wholeness, and the quiet strength to begin again. Her story is a testament to the power of surrender and the beauty of becoming.

In "Letting Go: Trusting God Through a Hard Season in Life," Melissa Lindsey opens her heart to readers as she recounts a season marked by struggle and spiritual stretching. In learning to release what she could not control, she found God's presence in new and unexpected ways. This chapter is a tender reminder that even when letting go feels impossible, God holds what we cannot—and walks with us into what's next.

Karen Joy Cummings closes the collection by beautifully reframing the concept of an "empty nest," declaring that wherever God dwells, there is always fullness. Through poetic reflection and personal story, she invites readers to see their homes and hearts as sacred places still filled with love, purpose, and divine presence. Her words are a comforting embrace for any woman wondering what remains when so much seems to have changed.

Chapter 1

Beauty, Grace and Order: Creating a Home to Nourish your Next Chapter

By Karen Griffith

"HE HAS MADE EVERYTHING BEAUTIFUL IN ITS TIME. HE HAS ALSO SET ETERNITY IN THE HUMAN HEART; YET NO ONE CAN FATHOM WHAT GOD HAS DONE FROM BEGINNING TO END."
ECCLESIASTES 3:11 (NIV)

I came out of the womb with a love for home in my heart and a tape measure in my hand. I have always been captivated by good design and craved beautiful spaces. I had an intuitive feeling that we were created to live with comfort, beauty, and joy. That we were meant to live in peaceful places to be nurtured, and vibrant places to be inspired. That we were made for celebration.

I was on a mission to create this in my life, but I also questioned the "whys." It all *sounds* so good, but really, why does it matter? Are all the people in the magazines with gorgeous homes showcasing festive celebrations fully alive and satisfied? Does a beautiful living room *really* make for a happy life?

You probably know the answer to that. It's taken almost a lifetime for me to figure out, but what I have landed on is that home, and the feelings home evokes—joy, contentment, peace—is a blend of beauty, grace, and order. A home needs to fit your unique needs. It takes time, love, and methodical tending. It needs your patience and presence. True beauty comes with age. It is solidified and wrapped in memory and experience. A beautiful home is those things, too.

I remember believing I would do it so well. With all the wrong in my childhood, I had learned and was going to do it better. I would be loving and patient and create the perfect environment. With a design degree and plenty of therapy behind me, I would create a lovely home even on a tight budget. It would nurture curiosity and creativity. It would welcome friends and family and be a sweet container of memories. Anything wrong could be righted here.

Plus, I was much older than my mom when she had me, and her family legacy of alcoholism was not passed on. I was healed, whole, and more mature. I would know all the right things to do and say.

That confidence lasted until the moment I gave birth.

Immediately after my first was born, I had an extraordinary sense of compassion for my own mother, a sense of love and forgiveness, and sorrow all at the same time. So much to be responsible for. So much to learn.

Months earlier, while driving to visit my mom in the hospital, we got stuck behind a school bus stopping at every country house on the two-lane highway. Just as we'd gather a little speed, the brake lights would go on, and we'd watch another little backpack-laden kiddo run across the road to their home. I looked at my belly, unable to fathom that my own baby would someday wear that big of a backpack, much less be gone for an entire day of school.

But she did. Both of them did. And now I sit wondering where those last twenty years have gone, and how they could possibly be entering adulthood.

They told me it would go by fast. And it did.

But they didn't tell me how the sweet and simple moments would be so much more than sweet and simple, that the joy would be more satisfying than I ever would have imagined. They also didn't tell me how I would be blindsided with loss, that in the same three-year period I was married and had two babies, I would lose my mom to ovarian cancer, that there would be more heartache to come, and a great deal of failure along the way. That, no, indeed, I would neither be the perfect mother, nor create the perfect home.

Nice thought, though.

I did the best I could. There *were* lots of joyful times. I *did* create magical spaces. I *did* care for and nurture my family. I made every effort to set up for whatever stage my family was in, growing ever more comfortable with the reality that my perfect solutions for toy and book organization were usually outdated before they were fully implemented. I tried to record as much as I could through journals and photos, and scrapbooks of schoolwork and art. I tried to be present. I spent way too much time (attempting to) organize Legos.

And I spent a lot of time on the floor playing, having messy tea parties, and building forts.

My home was indeed lovely, but not for the reasons I had pictured.

Now they are off, with their own stories, their own struggles, and their own ways of bringing healing and beauty to the world.

And so are your kids. And you did the best you could, too. Your home *was* lovely. And now it's time for the next chapter. It's time to breathe, process, rest, and maybe even grieve. It's time to find ways to honor your memories while creating space for your next stage. It's time to consider how beauty, grace, and order can bring fulfillment to your home and life now.

Beauty

> *"I see beauty as a thin place, a place where the veil temporarily rises and we glimpse something of the Eternal."* *-Janet Hagberg*[1]

Pretty succinct.

Beauty inspires us and completes us. Our desire for it is inbred. Think of your eye resting on a colorful landscape or a vase of flowers; a lovingly set table, an inviting sofa filled with patterned pillows, a piece of art that strikes you with its color, form, or design. I believe that the elements and principles of design are nature's divinely inspired ideas; a gift of God to create beauty for our well-being and pleasure.

1 Janet Hagberg, "An Oasis of Beauty, Hope, and Healing," *JanetHagberg.com*, June 2020, http://www.janethagberg.com/beauty.html.

They were born in the Garden of Eden, our original home, our first source of inspiration and satisfaction.

If you were to create your own "Garden of Eden," what would it look like? What does it look like now? Maybe you just got back from dropping your last one off at college? Maybe you still have piles of laundry that didn't make the cut or piles of pictures you went through for the graduation party? Maybe you have the same furniture or pictures out that were there on that first day of kindergarten? Maybe you have never had the energy or the time or the bandwidth to give it any thought?

We recently finished our basement and embarked on a year-long project of "finishing things and doing all the things we always wanted to do but never had the time or money or energy to do until now." After the busyness of kids' schedules and appointments, parent meetings, and coordinating calendars, I wanted to take a fresh look at how our home will be used in the future. I want our home to tell our story, bring us joy, and welcome others. The first step, as always, is determining how the space will be used. What do I want to do? How will I (and my husband) spend our time now?

I need a space where the TV will not dominate, but rather, there are comfy chairs to plop down on and invite conversation. I want a comfortable *white* sofa to host my friends, appliances that I enjoy using, quiet places to work and read, and a space for my kids and their friends to hang out separately if they want to when they *are* home.

I want things to feel cohesive and put together. I want to see snippets of our lives over the years through photos and art collected on vacations, but I want a freshness, too.

My mom had a mink coat. I remember the Christmas that she got it, and how excited she was to put it on. She sat with her martini on the sofa and smiled a playful, smug smile. The coat hung in my closet for years after she died. Despite its warmth and the fact that it was an elegant dressy coat, and I didn't have one of those, it wasn't my style, and I wouldn't wear it. Even while she was still alive, we talked about what could be made out of it. She had one granddaughter, and another one on the way, so maybe some type of doll coats? A stuffed animal?

We never got to the project before she died, and the coat was just taking up space. Until it occurred to me that I could have some pretty fabulous pillows made from it. I found a reluctant seamstress to do the work, and I assured her that whatever she created, I would be happy with. Better some funny-looking pillows than a coat just occupying space in the closet.

She got three pillows out of the coat, and they are the coziest pillows I own. They are an elegant and fluffy reminder of my moms's warm hugs. The warm hugs she gave in the twenty-five years she lived in sobriety. They make me smile. They help me honor my past and think joyfully and hopefully of the future.

Maybe you are staying put in your home, or starting fresh in another. Either way, consider how you want to spend your time and what you want to invite into your life. How can your space reflect who you are now? How do you want to feel here? What do you want each room to do for you? What is beautiful to you in your current spaces, and what is not? What would make it more beautiful for you? Is there something from your past that can be transformed to give you hope and joy for your future?

This all might not come to you right away. You might need some time to figure out what you want to do and how you want to feel in each room. You might, like us, just want to finish things to "good enough," be done, and enjoy all the beauty you have created so far. But you get to decide now. You don't have to wait. What delights you, and how can you bring it into your home?

Grace

Grace is the anchor of a home, an extension of love. It's the salt, the seasoning, the warm smile. It stems from gratitude and shows up as acceptance. Grace gives us the capacity to meet others where they are without letting others' stories define our happiness.

Beauty without grace is empty.

When life feels like it has gone by too fast, like you want a do-over, like you failed and wish you knew then what you know now, remember the power in gratitude and acceptance. You've made it this far, you raised a family, and you created memories. With every hat you've worn over the years, you've given a God-made part of you. Write down everything you are grateful for, so that you remember. Make it a daily practice. Then trust. Trust God with your kids and their stories. They were knit in yours or another's womb by God. They will have a lifetime of experiences you could not possibly orchestrate, but you can still be their home.

I remember the stroller rides and my daughter gazing up at a Weeping Willow tree for the first time, something I imagined was magical for her. And her eventually learning the name of the tree. I am grateful for all the stroller rides, that I was there for the dance recitals and gymnastics meets, band concerts, the field trips, and the picnics. I am grateful for the joy of all of those little moments. I am grateful for every smile I witnessed, for every time I held them and soothed their fears and feelings. For every time I saw them delight in something new.

Things didn't always go as planned. People and families are flawed. Much of the time, we are on autopilot, rarely showing up intentionally as our best selves. But we weren't put on earth "finished," we were put on earth "just getting started."

Grace in my home in this season means taking a fresh look at both myself and my family, who we are now, and what we need. There may be past hurts that need to be addressed, but there is also a lot of good to look forward to. So to be strong for my family and future, I need to take care of myself, which will include a new level of routines and taking care of my health.

Not too long ago, I enjoyed a spring break in Palm Springs in a wheelchair. I had injured my back, and against the advice of my doctor, plodded on with my plans. I brought plenty of pain pills and a deflated exercise ball, and committed to doing my physical therapy exercises like it was my job.

I really don't recommend that. But, I will say that I was determined to enjoy it and I did. My family patiently helped me along. And I learned that I needed to take better care of myself if I wanted to prevent this from ever happening again. Once I got strong enough, I recommitted to exercise. I want to welcome my family with joyful energy. I want the strength for all that is to come.

What does grace in your home look like to you now? Can you accept yourself as you are now, so you can do the same for others? What do you want for yourself? How do you want to be with your family? Are there comforting rituals to continue or establish? What good can you focus on? Can you trust the good that is to come?

A home that extends grace is palpable. Your job is not done; your kids just need you in different ways now. They get to grow up, and you get to move forward. And it starts with you loving yourself right here, right now.

Order

I mentioned that we recently finished our basement. What I didn't mention was the twenty-plus years of stuff we went through and moved along in order to do that. My husband was a teacher for thirty-seven years, and had as much of his teaching "stuff." I am a packrat and spent several years hunting estate sales for cool stuff and "someday" projects. It's still hard for me to let go of some of it. I also never really edited my kids' schoolwork or artwork, or any other note or newsletter they may have brought home from school.

So, much of that was piled on the ping pong table and spilling onto the floor. We committed to doing whatever it took to clear that space so we could finally finish it. I had tubs and tubs of holiday decorations, many I didn't even like or use. I had half-finished crafts and broken things waiting to be fixed. We even had our kids' old beds, just in case there were slumber parties that we might schlep them up the stairs for. The slumber parties happened, but the schlepping did not. Way too much work.

It was time to move things along.

I gained a new perspective on "things" in the one year that I attended nine funerals: a friend my age, a child, family members, and family friends. That was a few years *after* I lost my mom, and several years *before* I lost both my dad and my only brother. That's a lot of loss. It brought me to a new viewpoint on "things." It's ok to let go of your loved one's things that don't necessarily make *you* smile, and to find new homes for things that may hold more meaning for others than for you. I am working on curating a single tub for each of my family members—for their papers, photos, and memorabilia, and to find meaningful ways to honor them. Crowding my life with their things won't do that.

What does order look like to you now? Are you hanging onto others' things? Are you letting things pile up? You get to choose now. You get to winnow it down. You get to let go of what has no meaning for you and projects you have no desire to finish, in order to create space for what you want to fill your life with now.

Maybe you've never had a chance to go through each drawer and closet and shelf, one at a time, and clean it out? Do you have a home for everything you own? If you can't find a home for it, do you need it? When your space is organized, there is a lightness and simplicity to your life. If you think it's too late for that, that you have too much stuff, it's not, and you don't. Take the time you need to do this. It won't be easy, but cultivate this skill so that you can live it and enjoy it. Who knows, maybe you can teach it to your grandchildren? Do you remember how fast those last twenty years went? The days of grandchildren might be here before you know it.

Once you've straightened out your drawers and closets and determined the projects you want to finish and those you want to let go of, give your house a good, thorough cleaning. Hire out if you can. You might discover your home is already everything you want!

Whatever our stories, whatever baggage we brought to our own families, whatever events that blindsided us, God has, and always has had a plan. You and your family are not exempt from God's redemption story—you are a part of it. I grew up in an alcoholic and drug addicted home. Some years in the middle weren't necessarily pretty, graceful, or orderly. But my earliest years and my young adult life tell a different story. Those were the years my mom *did* create a lovely home. There were festive holiday dinners with old China in a new house. There were cozy nights by the fire, long conversations, joyful laughter, new adventures, shopping trips and vacations, and outdoor discoveries. There was grace and healing and beauty, all in its time. *These* are the years still ahead of me ... and you.

So, what does it mean to create a home now? How do you want to grow? What do you want your home to be for you at this time? Now that it may be quieter? Now that there may be more spaces and more hours to fill? How will you honor your stories and create a space you love for all that is to come?

Next Steps

I invite you to visit divinelefse.com to download your free copy of "Simple Ways to Create Your Garden of Eden" and sign up for "*a little dose of divine lefse.*" a weekly newsletter filled with practical tips and inspiration for living out beauty, grace, and order in your home.

Chapter 2

Be On Your Way: Sowing Seeds of Purpose

By Brenda Woomer

"THE LORD SAID TO SAMUEL, 'HOW LONG WILL YOU MOURN FOR SAUL, SINCE I HAVE REJECTED HIM AS KING OVER ISRAEL? FILL YOUR HORN WITH OIL AND BE ON YOUR WAY; I AM SENDING YOU TO JESSE OF BETHLEHEM. I HAVE CHOSEN ONE OF HIS SONS TO BE KING." 1 SAMUEL 16:1 (NIV)

As I stood in the back of the garage, I could feel the tears slowly well up. Why would these dill seedlings sprouting in the back of the garage cause such an emotional response in me? Although my friends would be the first to confirm the fact that I am a "crier," even this would catch them off guard. *It's Dill, Brenda. Dill that you planted. What is going on with you?* I was grateful to be alone as I stood staring at the sight. I needed a minute to process the message God was whispering to my momma heart. It was a message of purpose I had been longing to hear, but didn't realize how much I needed. While I looked for direction through neon signs, God chose to send sprouting seeds.

I was not prepared for the mix of emotions that would arrive as I watched my boys become young men and leave home. Four years ago, seasons changed quickly for my family. It was May when Seth, my oldest of two sons, graduated from college. A couple of weeks later, Jesse, the younger of the two, graduated from high school. Less than a month after that, Seth was married. We celebrated the accomplishments of our boys. We were filled with joy and gratitude as our family began to grow. But there was also uncertainty in this uncharted territory as my nest started to empty. One year later, Jesse transferred to a university five hours from home. And then there were two: My husband and I. In a home that seemed way too quiet. What was this new life?

I suppose it is the goal of most parents, right? To raise children up in the way they should go (Proverbs 22:6, NIV). It does say "... they should go," Not "... they should stay and remain unchanged, immature boys forever, so you feel like you have purpose and maintain control." My husband and I taught our sons as best we knew how, and then sent them out to do the very best they could do with what they learned. I will be the first to admit that neither the teaching nor the sending were done perfectly. But the end goal was to reach a point where we would release control of the day-to-day decisions that awaited them, from choosing a school or a house to selecting a job or a spouse. We prayed and trusted God would fill in the spaces where we dropped the ball in the teaching. No one prepared me for the wrestling that comes with the sending. My purpose and mindset had been so intertwined with raising my boys, and now, as we released them, I wasn't sure what to hold on to. I felt unsteady and uncertain. Even though I knew it was right, I was not ready.

Some of my happiest moments to date are the simple ones. The sound of a voice ringing out from the bathroom as music blared and the shower ran always made me smile. I even have audio recordings tucked away that I occasionally listen to. Evenings with my people sitting around our table. The familiar laughter and ornery banter fill my joy cup like little else does. It was a regular occurrence when the boys were young. I miss it. I miss the time I had with them as I'd drive them to school each morning. "This is the day ..." I would begin, and they would respond one by one, "that the Lord has made ..." then "[I] will rejoice and be glad in it" (Psalm 118:24, NKJV). Although as they got older, the responses came begrudgingly (anyone else remember the teenage years?), it is a memory I hold dear.

As moms, so much of our time, thoughts, and actions are centered around caring for our children. Years filled with telling bedtime stories and listening to their sweet prayers. Hours spent helping with homework and laboring over laundry. Monitoring chore charts and rationing screen time. Sporting events and suppers on the run. Breaking up fights, but also hugging tightly. When time is filled with a list of to-dos that include our children, questions of what God is calling a mom to do can be answered with a quick glance at the list. Moms live out a large portion of their purpose with each nose wiped, cut bandaged, meal cooked, and dish put away. Having successfully transported all the people to all the places and fitting in all the games possible, there is a joy–a peace even–that you have carried out the thing God has asked you to do.

But now?

Now, that list has whittled down to the laundry, though the piles are smaller. The many random hugs in the kitchen while trying to get a meal on the table have been replaced by hugs of hello and goodbye. The list dwindles, and the mom-taxi isn't needed. Supper is for two, or maybe for you it's just one. Purpose becomes less clear. At least it did for me. When my table wasn't filled daily, and the voices didn't echo down the hall, I found myself trying to figure out where to focus, what to change, where to remain, and what to do next.

If God's word is true, and I believe that it is, then He has a plan and a purpose for each of us that was determined even as we were formed in our mother's womb (Psalm 139:13-16, paraphrased). I am not one to proclaim that there is just one purpose you are supposed to fulfill, and if you miss it, well then, too bad. I believe God places purpose within us to be carried out as we walk the path He sets before us. We all have a calling to love well and serve Him. But we are each unique, so the purpose and path will look different based on the varied gifts and talents He gives.

When the path I was walking out seemed to end, the questions began. Maybe you are asking similar things. Does this require something brand new of me? Is it okay to mourn what I am missing from the years of filled tables, loud laughter, and songs flowing from the shower at 11 pm? What am I supposed to do now that the sending years are here, and I'm not sure how to walk out these next steps? Where is God's path leading me now? What do I put my seemingly empty hands to?

Tears fall now as I allow myself to feel the emotions that accompanied the questions. With time, I was able to name what I was facing: Grief. It was the mourning of what was but is no more. It is so important to acknowledge it as such. This grief is what I was not prepared for. I was not aware that joy would be harder to find when the raising up transitioned to sending out. I was mourning. I felt sad and stuck. Melancholy and meandering.

And then two years ago, my husband and I moved in with his mother due to a medical incident that prompted the need for us to be present in her day-to-day living. She is the sweetest mother-in-law that I could have asked for. Her home sits on the banks of the Ohio River. The sunrise reflecting in the water each morning is a beautiful reminder of His constant presence. But even though I am grateful for these things, this is not my home. My nest is not only empty, but I am living in someone else's. This is not the empty nest adjustment I had envisioned, and it added another layer to the pain of grieving as my boys became young men.

It was in this season of mourning that I found Samuel's story in 1 Samuel 16. I don't remember what led me to this chapter and verse, but I am certain God meant for me to find it in this season of grief. I pray you will find it was meant for you, too.

If you are unfamiliar with Samuel of the Bible, let me give you a little back story. He was a prophet and judge chosen by God to anoint Saul as Israel's first king. Samuel served as a mentor and advisor to King Saul for over eighteen years. Eighteen years of advising, correcting, and encouraging. Sound familiar? But eventually, God told Samuel that He was rejecting Saul as king due to Saul's evil ways. It was time to anoint a new king. Samuel obeyed God and parted ways with Saul. It was the end of an era. But 1 Samuel 15:35 tells us that Samuel mourned for Saul during this shift in seasons. I can sympathize with his grief; Can you? Samuel spent years pouring into the life of someone God had placed in his path. He spent time with him. He prayed earnestly for him. He rejoiced in his successes and felt the sting of his failures. Samuel's purpose—his calling—was to serve God by serving Saul. And then that purpose ended. This is where 1 Samuel 16:1 jumps off the page at me.

> *"The Lord said to Samuel, 'How long will you mourn for Saul, since I have rejected him as king over Israel? Fill your horn with oil and be on your way; I am sending you to Jesse of Bethlehem. I have chosen one of his sons to be king.'"* (1 Samuel 16:1, NIV)

How long will you mourn? Fill your horn with oil. Be on your way.

How long will you mourn ...

There is no judgment in these words. There is no condemnation. In fact, I find grace and comfort here. God is acknowledging that the grief Samuel is experiencing is real. There is permission to pause and mourn what has ended. Permission to grieve the loss of something you will never get back. Time to remember. Time to let go.

I don't know if you are a momma of littles who just sent their last child off to kindergarten and you miss having her with you all day, every day. You miss hearing every little laugh and word. Or maybe your teenager just drove out of the driveway by himself for the very first time. Daily routines are about to change. Or maybe you are like me, with one son married and one recently engaged and graduating from college. You will never have your children living together under one roof again. Whatever it was that is no more, you have permission to grieve the loss of it. Acknowledge the grief. Take time to mourn the loss. Brenda Yoder writes, "While challenging, grief is also a testament to our capacity for love and connection. It reflects the depth of our experiences and the richness of our lives."[2] Be grateful that there was something wonderful worth mourning.

How long will you mourn ...

The question alone prompts the consideration—what is a reasonable time to mourn? The question also implies an end to the mourning. There is a difference between grieving and mourning. While grieving is more of an inward feeling and emotional response, mourning is the outward expression of that grief. Mourning is displayed in our behavior and actions. It could also be seen in our lack of action. God is telling Samuel that it is time to consider how his actions have reflected his grief. God is prompting him to move from standing still in the memory of the past to stepping out with a mindset on purpose.

In my grief, my mourning had me feeling stuck. The will to move forward was lacking. God was asking me the same question he had asked Samuel. How long will you mourn? He was reminding me that my purpose was not lost with the things I was grieving. What had passed had been preparing

---

2 Brenda Yoder, "Light in the Shadows: Coping With Grief," *Brendayoder.com*, 1 Oct. 2024, https://brendayoder.com/coping-with-grief-brenda-l-yoder/. Accessed 11 Apr. 2025.

me for what is next. And it was time to listen to His voice propelling me forward.

Is it time to adjust your focus and prepare your heart to move forward? Doing so does not mean grief will end and you'll never long for those morning routines, Saturday soccer games, or late-night talks on the couch. Moving forward just requires us to carry the grief rather than allowing it to cover us until we end up as an unmovable mess. Brenda Yoder continues, "As we move forward, let's carry our grief not as a weight that holds us down, but as a reminder of our shared humanity. In acknowledging our losses, we open ourselves to new beginnings and unexpected blessings."[3] Moving forward does not mean you will stop missing the things you have loved about the season of life that is ending. It just means there is a time to listen to God's loving voice beckoning you forward into something new, prepared for you. It is time to set your mind on His purpose for you.

Fill your horn with oil …

"A horn?" you ask. Like a trumpet? No. But wouldn't that be fun! Although there were rams' horns during Samuel's time used as a trumpet or "shofar," this passage is referring to something else. This type of horn was a vessel used as a container. For Samuel specifically, it was a vessel filled with anointing oil. Samuel's horn carried the oil that anointed Saul as king. It is interesting that Samuel was told to use the same vessel he'd used before. He was being asked to fill it back up and get ready to use it again for the next assignment God was preparing. Samuel was being asked to transition

3 Yoder, "Light in the Shadows."

from mourning the past to moving toward the future. And the thing required in between? Being filled.

I think it is important to recognize that God's instruction to fill this horn with oil required a response from Samuel. God had displayed His power to Samuel enough in the past that it would not have been a surprise if God said, "I have filled your horn with oil and it is ready to go." But no. This next step required Samuel's cooperation with God. Samuel needed to find the oil, prepare the vessel, and then fill it up. God has a pattern throughout the Bible of allowing His children to participate in His plans. Something miraculous happens as we partner with Him.

Fill your horn with oil ...

As I read this passage and considered God's instructions, I knew, despite my empty feeling, He was nudging me to begin the transition from mourning to moving forward. In response, I took the first steps to fill my horn the best way I knew how—by seeking Him. For years, I have had the privilege of sitting in the den of my dear friend's home on a regular basis. We have studied God's word and done life together with a group of women who will listen to your heart, cheer for your achievements, and encourage you when you need it. But more than anything, they compel you to seek Him first. It is a gift I do not take for granted. It was at this Bible study, while I was struggling to step out of mourning, that someone asked each of us, "What is giving you life in this season?" I wrestled with this question. In my emptiness, I had no response. But deep down, I knew the answer was worth pursuing. God was asking me again to consider how I could fill my horn with oil. I knew that if I allowed Him to point out the life-giving things He had already placed in my life, I could use those things to be filled again and prepare for whatever God was calling me to. So I asked Him to help me notice life-giving moments.

The Bible study was the first thing that came to mind as I sought to fill my horn. It was giving me life even when I felt I had nothing to give. So, I kept going. Even as I entered a season of melancholy, I made it a priority to dig into His word. Often, I did not feel like I was learning much of anything from reading. Journaling seemed to dry up. Things that gave me so much joy in the past simply felt like a box checked off my list. But I kept reading. I kept pursuing. I would write what few words came to mind, or I would simply write out a verse, hoping it would spark something within me. And I'd do it again another day. I begged Him to show me what He had planned for me. I trusted in His character. I knew He was with me even if I didn't perceive it. I learned that His word and truth were vital for my filling.

My husband, Tom, was another response to the life-giving question. In a season of hard transitions, I cherished the patience and comfort he offered me in abundance. His understanding, kind words, and surprise date nights reassured my heart that whatever lay ahead, we would face it together. As I watched him gently care for his mom, I was reminded of why I first fell in love with him. We have been married for over 30 years, but in this season especially, his love was filling me up.

My best friend, Lisa, was also at the top of my life-giving list. When our sons became best friends in kindergarten, our friendship began as well. She is the friend God knew I needed from our first conversation on that park bench at a school picnic. She provided deep conversations and the best belly laughs that were medicine for empty spaces in me that needed filling.

Slowly, day by day, with all these life-giving things, my horn was being filled. I barely recognized it as it happened. It reminds me of my favorite line from Lisa Whittle's book, *Put Your Warrior Boots On*: "We will never just one day wake up warriors. We will prepare for the day we need to become one and find out we already are."[4] As I was filling my horn with my Bible and journal in hand, in that den, listening to the Holy Spirit and wise women, I was being prepared. Not by my own doing, but by His undoing of my preconceived ideas of what my life should look like. As I filled my horn with the love of my spouse and support from my friend, I was encouraged. God was using the familiar things in my life to move me into the new things of His plan. He was healing my heart and redirecting my focus from what I was missing to what He was preparing. I was ready for the next steps. I just didn't know what they were. The time for mourning was ending. My horn was being filled, and it was time to be on my way.

If you are unsure what it would look like to fill your own horn with oil, I hope you will begin by reading the Bible. Maybe that is a new thing for you. Perhaps it is a habit you've set aside because grief has gotten in the way. I understand. I have been there. All I can promise is that there is an unexplainable filling that happens when you read the words of the One who knows you and loves you more than you can

---

4 Lisa Whittle, *Put Your Warrior Boots On* (Harvest House Publishers, 2017), 101.

imagine. He will fill you. Then begin to take notice of things that fill you up. The life-giving things. The familiar things—a spouse, a friend, or a walk in the woods. Allow God to use these things to fill you. So you too can be on your way.

Be on your way ...

God only gave Samuel a small glimpse of what moving forward meant. A new king was going to be anointed. Samuel knew the direction to travel, but could not see the entire picture God had planned. In fact, he didn't even know the name of the new king. Notice this was not some strange, unlikely, brand-new mission. It was familiar. It was the same calling, redirected, with new oil and new outcomes. New lessons to be learned and new people to pour into. Same mission. New journey. There was uncertainty in the journey, but Samuel had God's promise: "I will show you what to do" (1 Samuel 16:3, NIV). And because he had witnessed God's faithfulness and reliability, Samuel went, carrying the horn that he had filled, and trusting the One sending him.

Moving forward does not mean you have everything figured out. Samuel did not know the details. I certainly did not know where to find purpose with this empty nest. I considered dreams I had before I became a mother, as well as new dreams that grew over the past twenty-five years. The desire to sing as part of a worship team had never faded. In fact, I felt that was a purpose God placed within me. I had also been in a few musicals before my sons were born and loved it. Maybe that is what moving forward would look like. I started watching for musical auditions at my local actor's guild. I didn't know which dreams to chase. And I had no peace to pursue any of these things.

God told Samuel He would tell him what to do. I held on to that same promise and finally surrendered, bringing my questions to God. I came to Him, pen in hand, with my questions and my list of possibilities. I am so grateful for a God who is not far off and invites us to come when we are weary. You can take a lesson from me and just jump to this step first. Bring your questions to Him. Make the lists. Take an inventory of dreams, past and present. Consider what was, is, and could be. Then ask Him.

What goes?

What remains?

What are you adding?

What is my purpose in this season?

I asked these questions, believing He would at least show me which direction to walk. And He did. In time. Trust Him to do the same for you.

Be on your way...

I continued asking God to give me direction as I attempted to move forward and find purpose. It was in a Sunday morning message that the following verse caught my attention. I had read the verse before, but that day it stood out to me, and I wrote it down.

> *"Those who sow with tears will reap with songs of joy. Those who go out weeping, carrying seed to sow, will return with songs of joy, carrying sheaves with them."* Psalm 126:5-6 (NIV)

I resonated with moving forward while still weeping. It was how I was moving forward in this season of an empty nest. These verses suggest that even while we are weeping, there is still work to be done. That work is to sow seeds, which will one day bring joy in the harvest.

The day I heard this verse in a Sunday sermon was the same day I stood crying at the sight of my dill seedlings. The seed talk in this verse had piqued my interest. I am a homesteader wanna-be. Equipped with this aspiration and much research, I was sowing my own seeds to plant in our garden. I planted all kinds of seeds—tomatoes, peppers, flowers, and of course, the dill. What I was learning with my very official YouTube education was that different types of seeds require different amounts of time to germinate and sprout. Unfortunately, I planted all my seeds at one time, without knowing the specifics of timing for my newfound hobby. I just stuck them all in the dirt and hoped for the best. In fact, I had basically been neglecting them after they were planted. I knew what I had sown. I just had not tended to them like an experienced homesteader would have known to do. On this Sunday, I walked into the garage expecting to see only dried-up dirt to be tossed out. But instead, I found the dill, reaching for the light from the nearby window.

I use dill each year for canning pickles. I hate pickles, by the way. But guess who loves them: My family. I only planted this dill because my family loves the dill pickles I make from our cucumber harvest. And here, growing in my mismatched seed-packed dirt was the herb I grew solely to serve my family. And it was at the sight of this dill that God caught me off-guard and whispered to my heart, "These are the seeds I am asking you to sow in this season. Sow into your family before anything else."

Serving my family has always been a huge part of my heartfelt purpose. God never asked me to change who I was or what I did. While I was watching for some brand-new mission, he was telling me to stick to my 'dill' and continue in this purpose that dwelt deep within me. Serving family would just look different now. It's like Samuel having the mission to anoint and serve a king. He had the same primary mission to carry God's anointing. He was just redirected in this new season. God was not telling me to stop pouring into the lives of my children. He was just asking me to transition from a leading role to a supporting role. He was asking me to include new people. Daughters-in-law. Grandchildren. Aging parents.

I will, as the Psalms passage states, go out weeping—because we've already established that I am a crier. But I will continue carrying seeds to sow. And the first seed is the family seed. Purpose does not end when your children leave your home, even if how that purpose is carried out does. Adjusting to the new expression of that purpose is how to take the next steps to be on your way.

Rather than daily talks at the dinner table, I will stay up until 11 p.m. on a Tuesday to chat with Jesse on the phone because we all know that is when he will be ready to open up and have the deep conversations. Or I will jump at the chance for Friday night dinner plans with Seth and his family because there are fewer things that bring me joy like spending an evening with them.

Rather than taking my boys to work with me like I did when they were young, I will happily leave work early to babysit the sweetest granddaughter on the face of the earth.

I will take my mother-in-law shopping on a Monday because it is sunny and too nice to be cooped up in the house any longer. I will sit with her and make sure all her bills are paid and in order.

I will take walks in the park with Tom on a Wednesday because our time alone with conversation and connection fuels my days and weeks. Hand in hand, I feel his strength and support as I do my best to offer the same.

These are the things I am sowing into now. This is what it looks like for me to be on my way. I will continue to sow seeds. Not just the dill that I talk of here, but other seeds as well, in their time. I will watch for growth and listen for His direction as I continue to walk on the path He has prepared, with the purpose He's provided. I don't know exactly what the harvest will look like, but I am catching a glimpse of it in my granddaughter's giggles. I will follow His leading and trust that I will return singing songs of joy.

He will tell me what to do. He will do the same for you.

Don't give in to the pressure of the question, "What is your purpose *now*?" Rather, consider how to continue carrying out the purpose God placed within you. Love well, and serve Him. I truly believe if you sow these seeds, you will receive a harvest at the right time for the right people. The key is to look around and see what seeds are growing this season and tend to them. For you, it could be seeds sown in self-employment or dreams placed on hold while raising children. It could be seeds of stories hidden in piles of journals waiting to be shared to encourage, entertain, or inspire others. Or maybe it is to reconnect with your spouse, traveling to places you've dreamed about for years.

What is your 'dill'? What is God nudging you toward in this season? Tend to that while carrying seeds to sow. Be on your way. I pray that you will return with songs of joy.

Next Steps

Grab a journal or sketchbook, take a walk, or sit quietly as you consider the following questions.

1) How long will you mourn? What are you mourning? Take time to acknowledge and name these things. As you make a list, mentally or on paper, allow space to remember and recognize the gift each thing was in its season.
2) Fill your horn with oil. What is giving you life today? Make an intentional decision to pursue things that have filled you in the past or bring hope today. Make a plan for reading His Word. It can be as simple as a verse or a chapter a day. Start somewhere.
3) Be on your way. What is your dill? Take your list to God. Ask the questions and watch for answers. Be open to new things, but do not despise the familiar. Where do you see growth in things you have sown into? Ask God to show you what to do.

Chapter 3

Who Are You: Finding Your Identity in Christ Alone

By Jane Harper DeLong

"YET TO ALL WHO DID RECEIVE HIM, TO THOSE WHO BELIEVED IN HIS NAME, HE GAVE THE RIGHT TO BECOME CHILDREN OF GOD." JOHN 1:12 (NIV)

Before my daughter even made it to the car, I could see that she had been crying. When she got in the car, she burst into tears and wailed, "I didn't get to go to recess today!" Ever the skeptical one, I asked what she had done to keep her inside. Her response both infuriated me and propelled me into a major life change.

Jennifer was a very smart five-year-old. She learned her ABCs at the tender age of two, and by three, she was reading simple words. By four, she was reading her children's books to her little brothers. When she started kindergarten that fall, she was reading at a second-grade level. It was now spring and time for statewide end-of-year assessments. Turns out that day, Jenn missed recess because the teacher used her as a tutor for a little boy who was still having trouble with his alphabet.

"I had to help Nate learn his ABCs because he will fail the test if he doesn't know them," was Jenn's reply that day.

This wasn't the first instance of Jennifer being used as a tutor, and the fact that she missed her recess in order to do the teacher's job made Mama Bear come out. In her five-year-old mind, she was being punished for knowing her ABCs. Punished for being smart.

If the boys had not been in the car with me that day, I would have gone straight to the teacher and let Mama Bear have her way! God has His way of saving us from ourselves! Instead of fighting with the teacher, I hit my knees and began praying about the education of our children. The Lord had already begun stirring a longing within me, and this incident with Jennifer brought that stirring to full force.

I am a teacher by trade, in passion, and in spiritual gifting, and not having an outlet for that was difficult. My husband and I had already begun discussing homeschooling, so when he heard what had happened that day, he was ready to do major research and make a decision. This was in the early 1990s, when very few people were homeschooling their children. Most people we talked to thought we were crazy for even thinking about it. But after about a month of researching, praying, and discussing, we decided this was indeed the road God wanted us to take. I spent that summer gathering materials and making plans. When September rolled around, we started our homeschool experience, and I became known as "the homeschooling mom."

Fast forward twenty years. Our youngest was finishing up her freshman year of high school when she told us she would really like to go to school outside our home for the rest of her high school years. This thought both frightened me and excited me, but soon the fright gave way to fretting and excitement to emptiness. What was I supposed to do now? For twenty years, I had wrapped my identity up in being "the homeschooling mom." Those final three years of Amanda's schooling were spent with me searching for meaning in my days. I had no idea who I was without the label I had worn for so long.

During those years, our nest began slowly emptying as the older kids started getting married or going away for college or work. When Amanda decided to go to college outside our state, my life was sent into a tailspin of confusion, depression, and aimlessness. Until my friend Tina made the comment one day: "Jane, your identity is not being a homeschooling mom. Your identity is being a child of God."

As I pondered those words, I realized I did not have a good grasp on what identity really is or on what being God's child really meant. I did what every good student does: I began delving into God's Word to see what He says about my identity. The more I studied, the more I realized that all my life I had tied my identity to three things: what I did, my relationships with others, and what I looked like. Turns out our identity doesn't have anything to do with those things!

I had placed my identity in what I did: I homeschooled, I was a wife, a mom, a daughter, a sister, a friend. I also placed my identity in what I looked like: I was tall, a little too heavy, and wore glasses. While these things do identify me to others, they are not who I am.

I had spent all those years defining myself through a worldly lens. This is all too common among women. We hang our identity hat on what the world says we are, rather than what our Heavenly Father says about us. The Biblical Counseling Coalition explains the difference between worldly identity and Christian identity this way: "While worldly identity defines who a person is according to self or others, Christian identity defines who a person is according to the Creator. While worldly identity keeps people focused on worldly things, Christian identity drives believers' focus toward heavenly things."[5] As Christians, our identity is not in what we do but in Whose we are. The Bible is very clear on who we are if we have accepted Jesus as Lord and Savior of our lives. John 1:12 tells us we are God's children; THIS is our identity. As God's Children, we are adopted, accepted, and affirmed.

Adopted: Who's Your Daddy?

We all have a biological father, whether he was a good and present daddy or one who abandoned us. We associate our feelings about God as our Father with the feelings we have toward our biological father. The thing is, our feelings are fallen and they lie. The Bible tells us that if we have been saved by faith in Jesus, then we have been adopted into God's family.

Adoption is a legal transaction that takes place when someone desires to take on the parental duties of a child who is not biologically theirs. Before the adoption is final, several requirements must be met.

5 Jeemin Moon, "Christian Identity: Worldly Identity vs. Christian Identity," *Biblical Counseling Coalition*, 5 Apr. 2024, https://www.biblicalcounselingcoalition.org/2024/04/05/christian-identity-worldly-identity-vs-christian-identity/. Accessed 21 May 2025.

- The prospective parents must choose an adoption agency or decide to adopt a child they are fostering.
- A home study must be completed. This is a thorough assessment of the home and family environment of the prospective parents. In this assessment, it is decided if the parents can provide a loving, stable, and safe home for the child. This includes a full disclosure of the financial well-being of the family.
- An adoption petition is filed with the court. This is a formal request for permission to adopt the child.
- An adoption hearing is held in front of a judge. At the end of this hearing, when the judge slams his gavel down, the adoption is finalized. The parent/child relationship is permanently and legally established.

We can apply these same steps to our spiritual adoption.

- God chose us to be His children.

Ephesians 1:4-5 says: "Even before he made the world, God loved us and chose us in Christ to be holy and without fault in his eyes. God decided in advance to adopt us into his own family by bringing us to himself through Jesus Christ. This is what he wanted to do, and it gave him great pleasure" (NLT).

While all people are created by God in His image and loved by Him, He chooses to adopt those who come to Him through faith in Jesus.

- God provides a loving, stable, and safe place for us. He is "Jehovah Jireh, the LORD my provider." This is the name Abraham gave God in Genesis 22:14 (NIV) when God provided a ram for a sacrifice in place of Isaac. God provides what we need when we need it.

Jesus tells us in Matthew 6:26: "Look at the birds of the air; they do not sow or reap or store away in barns, and yet your heavenly Father feeds them. Are you not much more valuable than they?" (NIV)

Our identity as God's children assures that our needs will be met.

- Jesus filed an adoption petition for us the moment we asked Him to be our Lord and Savior.

Paul explained this to the Galatians this way: "So the law was our guardian until Christ came that we might be justified by faith. Now that this faith has come, we are no longer under a guardian. So in Christ Jesus you are all children of God through faith, for all of you who were baptized into Christ have clothed yourselves with Christ" (Galatians 3:24-27 NIV).

Jesus fulfilled the Law of Abraham and, in so doing, He signed the adoption petition for every person who comes to faith in God through Him. His blood is the formal request to adopt us into God's family.

- God gives us His Spirit as proof that our adoption is final.

"When you believed, you were marked in him with a seal, the promised Holy Spirit, who is a deposit guaranteeing our inheritance until the redemption of those who are God's possession—to the praise of his glory" (Ephesians 1:13b-14, NIV). We are in God's family the moment we put our faith in Jesus; He places His Holy Spirit in us as a seal, saying we are His. At the end of time, when God slams His gavel down in judgment, those with this seal will enter into eternal life as sons and daughters of the King.

Because we are God's adopted children, we have the right to call Him "Daddy." (See Galatians 4:4-7) He is our loving Father. Our adoption into His family is permanent and legally established because of the death, resurrection, and ascension of Jesus Christ.

When we have invested so much time into raising our children, it's easy to forget our children don't define us; our status with God defines us. Yes, we are moms, but more than that, we are God's daughters. He has adopted us into His family, and He calls us His. This fact never changes, no matter how many people may occupy our homes.

Accepted: What Must I Do?

So many of us spend our lives trying to win the approval of others when, if we are in Christ, we already have the approval of Almighty God. Honestly, all those years I wrapped my identity up in my homeschooling, I was trying to win the approval of other moms I knew who didn't homeschool. I wanted to be accepted by them. I wanted my children to be accepted into social groups without being thought of as weird because they were homeschooled. We all have the need to be accepted, to belong.

In Matthew 3:13-17, we find the story of Jesus's baptism. Verse 17 says: "This is My beloved Son, in whom I am well pleased" (NKJV). God spoke these words as Jesus was coming out of the water. These are words of acceptance. So, **when** was Jesus accepted by God? Jesus had not yet spoken one word about God's Kingdom. He had not yet performed one miracle. He had not yet healed one person. He had not done one thing to earn God's acceptance. God accepted Jesus because of **Whose** He was, not what he had done.

The same is true for us. God accepts us before we have done anything in His name. God accepts us not because of what we have done but because of Whose we are.

Let's take a deeper dive into Ephesians 1:3-6. The NKJV translates these verses like this: "Blessed be the God and Father of our Lord Jesus Christ, who has blessed us with every spiritual blessing in the heavenly places in Christ, just as He chose us in Him before the foundation of the world, that we should be holy and without blame before Him in love, having predestined us to adoption as sons by Jesus Christ to Himself, according to the good pleasure of His will, to the praise of the glory of His grace, by which He accepted us in the Beloved."

In Christ, we have immediate and unconditional acceptance from God.

Who is God's Beloved? Matthew 3:17 tells us, Jesus. Who are we accepted through? Ephesians 1:6 tells us the Beloved, who is Jesus. The moment we turn to Jesus for salvation, we are accepted by God. We don't do anything to earn His acceptance except believe in His Beloved Son.

The verbs used in Ephesians 1:3-6 are in the past tense, meaning the action has already taken place. In verse 3, "has blessed" means it is already done. We are already blessed in Christ. God chose to accept those who believe in Jesus before the foundation of the world. The Bible is God's story of redemption, and before the world began, He was writing your story into His grand plan. In verse 5, "in Christ," we have already been adopted as God's children. An adopted child is a chosen child. It pleased God to make us part of His family. The Father took pleasure in us before the world began, before we ever spoke a fitting word, before we ever did one good deed. He takes pleasure in us now. He will always take pleasure in us, not because we are always pleasant or pleasing or good, but because of who we are in His Beloved Son.

Friend, I want you to know, you are accepted by God. But what exactly does that mean? The Bible tells us several things about God's acceptance of us:

- We are accepted in the Beloved the moment we accept the Beloved as our Lord, and we become God's children. (See John 1:12)
- Acceptance is an underserved gift of grace. (See Ephesians 2:8)
- We can't work to earn God's acceptance. (See Ephesians 2:9)
- God's love is measured by what it cost Him to accept us. It cost Him His Son. God accepts us because His Son took our place. (See Romans 5:8)

God doesn't save us and accept us because we are good enough. God saves and accepts us because He is perfectly good. Acceptance is the unconditional part of God's love for us.

We can't be "unaccepted" by making a mistake, committing a sin, or failing at something. God is not in the cancel culture. God is in the business of accepting those who accept His Son. So often in those 20+ years, I worried about what others thought about me. I allowed my children's behavior and their successes or failures to define me. I didn't realize that my identity wasn't tied to other people's acceptance of me. When I learned that I am an accepted child of God, I was able to begin living life free of worry about what others thought of me and my family. This knowledge enabled me to begin living victoriously in Christ.

What did this look like? It looked like total surrender. I learned to surrender all my fears and worries to God. Many days, this was a moment-by-moment surrender as I wrestled with those long-felt feelings of not being accepted by others. I surrendered my worries about what people thought of my children. I surrendered my need for the acceptance of people. I surrendered my thoughts of performance-based acceptance and began to find my acceptance in what God says about me. The more I did this, the more confidence I gained because I was learning to base my identity on God's acceptance of me rather than the acceptance of people. I realized no matter what I did, God accepted me and was pleased with me. This gave me the freedom to explore new interests and find new meaning in my days.

Acknowledging our acceptance in Christ is the difference between living a victorious Christian life and living a life in bondage to what others think of us. It's the difference between boldly living for Christ and cowardly living in fear. Knowing we are accepted in the Beloved empowers us to live a life worthy of God's calling as His children.

Do you know you are accepted by God? As you begin to watch your children grow up and leave your home, I hope you can see that your identity does not lie in what others think of you or your children. Your identity doesn't lie in others' acceptance of you or your children. No matter what you may find to do in these empty nest years, your identity remains the same: you are an accepted daughter of the King of kings, and He is well pleased with you.

Affirmed: Am I Worthy?

We all long to be worthy, to feel our lives count for something. Everyone wants to feel valuable to someone. In my years of being "the homeschooling mom," I placed my worth and value on how well my kids did in school, in their behavior, in their successes or failures. If they were doing well, I felt validated, worthy of respect from others. If they failed at something, I felt unworthy, as if I had failed in my life mission. My affirmation was tied up in my children's behavior and what other people thought of them, instead of what God says about me in His Word. In today's culture, it's popular to speak positive affirmations to yourself. But what does it really mean to affirm someone? Webster's 1828 Dictionary defines affirm: "to assert positively; to tell with confidence; to aver; to declare the existence of something; to maintain as true; opposed to deny."[6] According to this definition, to affirm someone is to declare the existence of something in their lives and to maintain it as true. But what is the truth? It's the age-old question. The culture in which we live tells us we can have our own truth, that there is no absolute truth. As Christians, we must reject this thought and stand firmly on the Holy Bible as absolute truth.

6 Noah Webster, "affirm," *Webster's 1828 American Dictionary of the English Language*, S. Converse, 1828, https://webstersdictionary1828.com/Dictionary/affirm. Accessed 17 Apr. 2025.

In my homeschooling days, I was maintaining what the world said about me as true. "She homeschools, so she's weird." "She homeschools, so she must be antisocial." "She homeschools, so she must think she's smarter than us." These are just a few of the thoughts the enemy placed in my mind as I went about my days teaching my children. Maybe people were thinking these things, and maybe they weren't. Either way, I felt I needed to prove myself to them in order to be counted worthy of their friendship. I went out of my way to fit in, sometimes going against what I knew was the godly thing to do. I was seeking affirmation from people rather than from God.

We've looked at Jesus's baptism and saw how God accepted Him simply because Jesus was His Son. God also affirmed Jesus. In Mark 9, we read the story of the transfiguration of Jesus. He took Peter, James, and John up a mountain to pray, and during that prayer time, Jesus was transformed into His divine glory. The Shekinah glory of God engulfed Him, and God's voice rang out, "This is my Son, whom I love. Listen to him!" (Mark 9:7, NIV) In these words, God once again affirmed Jesus as His Son, affirmed His love for Jesus, and affirmed Jesus's worth as someone to whom we should listen.

We all long to feel validated and worthy, but all too often, the world causes us to feel unworthy. As I've said, our feelings are fallen and they lie. When sin entered the world in the Garden, the feelings we had as perfect image bearers of God were altered. Our feelings of belonging became feelings of rejection. Our feelings of worthiness were transformed into feelings of unworthiness.

Feelings are like the check engine light on the dashboard of our car. When that light comes on, we know to take the car to a mechanic who can look under the hood and find out what's wrong. The mechanic has been trained to look for problems with the engine; he or she knows all the plugs and filters, and belts. They can find the problem and fix it with the right replacement part.

In Psalm 139, we learn that God knit each one of us together in our mother's womb. He knows us intimately. He knows our bodies and how each one works. He knows our brains and how we think. He knows our strengths and weaknesses. God knows everything about us. He created each one of us on purpose for a purpose. God is the Master Mechanic, and His Word has all the truth parts our broken feelings need in order to be "fixed."

So what are some of these truth-parts, Scriptures that affirm us as God's children? A great one to start with is 1 Peter 2:9: "But you are a chosen people, a royal priesthood, a holy nation, God's special possession, that you may declare the praises of him who called you out of darkness into his wonderful light" (NIV). In this one verse, God affirms us as chosen, royal, holy, and special. As His children, these are all part of our identity. When we place our identity in what the world says, like I did all those years, we will never be secure. Placing our identity in the fact that God sees us as chosen, royal, holy, and special enables us to move through the changes of life with confidence, knowing that He has a plan for each stage of our lives.

God affirms us as new creations in 2 Corinthians 5:17. I love the way the Amplified Bible (AMP) translates this verse.

"Therefore if anyone is in Christ [that is, grafted in, joined to Him by faith in Him as Savior], *he is* a new creature [reborn and renewed by the Holy Spirit]; the old things [the previous moral and spiritual condition] have passed away. Behold, new things have come [because spiritual awakening brings a new life]."

As God's children, we have been grafted into His family through our adoption. When God first created human beings, He created us in His image. Sin marred that image in all of us, but when we place our faith in Christ as Lord and Savior, God re-creates us. The word translated "new" in this verse is the word "kainos," which means "a new character of manhood, spiritual and moral, after the pattern of Christ."[7] Hanging our identity on the fact that we are made new in the pattern of Christ opens our eyes to see the new things God has for us as our children begin moving on in life. If we truly believe we are a new creation, then we are able to move through these changes with the assurance that God is leading us into His next best thing for us.

Another place God affirms us as His children comes from the mouth of Jesus in John 15 when He was teaching His disciples. In verse 15, Jesus calls us His friends, and in verse 16, He affirms once again that we are chosen and that we are appointed to bear much fruit. Raising our children is one of the places we are called to bear fruit. We've spent at least 18 years teaching, disciplining, and loving our children. That's a long time, and if we have multiple children, the time spent nurturing is even longer. Placing our identity in

7 W.E. Vine, *Vine's Complete Expository Dictionary of Old and New Testament Words* (Thomas Nelson, 1985), 431.

"momming" is easy to do; after all, we are always in demand, always needed by someone. Then suddenly the kids grow up and are less needy, and we find ourselves searching for something meaningful to spend our time on. However, if through the parenting years we have placed our identity in being a child of God, someone He considers His friend, someone appointed to bear lasting fruit, then we will not flounder when the kids start leaving the nest. As they leave, we will find new and exciting ways to bear the fruit God wants us to produce.

Eventually, this happened to me. As I began digging deeper into my identity in Christ, I realized that God still had work for me to do in His Kingdom. Raising my children was just part of His assignment for me. For all those years, my energy and focus went into raising and teaching our children. All too often, I made the mistake of placing my identity in what I did, but as I said earlier, my identity is not in what I do but in Whose I am. The difference between what we do and our identity lies in their definitions. What we do refers to the actions, roles, or activities we engage in. Our identity encompasses the characteristics, beliefs, and values that define who we are at the core of our being.

In a real sense, I suffered an identity crisis when my children were no longer in need of my help each day. Because my identity had been tied to what I did every day, the change of seasons that came with our nest emptying was very difficult for me. But as I learned to hang my identity on the fact that I am a child of God, those changes became easier. I learned that I didn't have to give up my passion for teaching. I learned that God could still use my love of teaching and my love for His Word by combining the two. He led me to teach women's classes at my church and lead women's retreats. Now I teach a weekly Bible study for moms of all ages, and my days are filled to overflowing with the joy that comes with bearing fruit for my Lord.

Sweet friend, as your nest empties, I pray you find your worth in being a child of God; if Jesus Christ is your Lord and Savior, that is what you are. There are no circumstances or changes in life that can alter your identity in Christ. However, if, like me, you've hung your identity on being a mom, you may end up blown and tossed by the changes an empty nest brings. Hang your hat on your true identity as God's child to ensure you don't suffer from "identity whiplash" as the seasons change in your life. In his book "Victory Over the Darkness," Neil T. Anderson wrote: "You must believe you are a child of God to live like a child of God."[8] Is this your belief, sweet friend? If so, I know you will find great joy in your empty nest years as you find new ways to bear fruit for the Lord!

Prayer for the Empty Nest Mom

Heavenly Father, You are Elohim, Creator God. You created each person with a unique purpose in mind. Raising a family has been such a big part of my purpose. But Lord, now the kids are grown and gone, and I want to know Your purpose for me in these empty nest years. Father, help me rest in the fact that I did a good work in raising them. Holy Spirit, enable me to realize my identity is in Christ alone and not in my children.

8 Neil T. Anderson, *Victory Over the Darkness* (Bethany House Publishers, 2013), 56.

Open my eyes to see the opportunities You place before me each day to serve You in new and exciting ways. As I have found freedom from being busy in my days, guide me to Your next fruit-bearing place as Your child. In Jesus' name, Amen.

Action: Now What?

In my office (which used to be a child's bedroom, yet another prop of having an empty nest!) I have a large mirror with the words God spoke to Jesus in Matthew 3:17 written on it. But my name is written in the verse, it reads: "Jane, You are my beloved daughter, with you I am well-pleased." I read this every morning and am reminded that God loves me simply because I am His, that is my identity. If you know Jesus, this is your identity as well.

Take an index card and write this verse with your name inserted. Or write it with a dry-erase marker on your bathroom mirror. Read these words daily and ask the Holy Spirit to remind you of your true identity when you begin feeling your worth is tied to what you do rather than Whose you are.

Chapter 4

Matriarch Mamas: The New Voice in Influencer Culture

By Kathleen A. Giles

"I AM REMINDED OF YOUR SINCERE FAITH, WHICH FIRST LIVED IN YOUR GRANDMOTHER LOIS AND IN YOUR MOTHER EUNICE AND, I AM PERSUADED, NOW LIVES IN YOU ALSO."
2 TIMOTHY 1:5 (NIV)

We bought our "forever" family home when my son was in kindergarten. As we toured the house prior to the sale, the realtor proudly showed us the two-story foyer with its sweeping oak staircase.

"Just imagine your daughter descending those steps in her wedding gown one day," she said.

"I can't picture it," I replied. "She's three."

"Just wait," the realtor warned. "You'll be surprised how fast that day will come."

Deep in the trenches of young motherhood, I could not envision the day my children would be capable of making their own lunches, much less getting married. And yet, other parents I knew had no trouble with that long-range perspective.

"Elizabeth turned nine this year," a fellow mama wrote in a long-ago Christmas letter. "It's hard to believe we are half-finished raising her."

Her phrasing caught me off guard. I thought, what happens when you are all finished? Do you retire?

That was not my concept of parenting. Nobody brings a newborn home from the hospital and says, "Okay, we have twenty years of work ahead of us, then we can retire."

But that's what society presumes when we get to the empty nest phase of life. Popular culture views motherhood as a job; therefore, launching adult children signals the end of our career. We are encouraged to embrace new work, often by focusing inward, on new leisure opportunities, or to pursue what we haven't had time, money, energy, or some other bandwidth to do when we had tiny humans depending on us.

For those who view motherhood as a calling, however, this perspective of the empty nest implies that our meaningful work is over. And perhaps, subtly, that we no longer have a place of influence in our children's lives.

Some moms find the tension between those two viewpoints hard to reconcile. So we struggle with "reclaiming ourselves" in the empty nest years. What's next? How do we find a new purpose? Do we even need a new purpose?

And then what?

The truth is, moms don't retire. Our tasks and responsibilities may change when our nest empties, but we do not stop being mothers. And while we can and should enjoy the freedom of this phase, we still have meaningful work to do in our families. As we embrace the life and purpose in our empty nest, it's okay to remember we still have influence in that sphere.

Let me show you how.

You Are an Influencer

First, let me start by saying I'm not sold on the "empty nester" label. To me, it conveys forlornness, a sad circumstance evoking vague pity, as though we are lacking something more than just our children living at home.

I prefer to call myself a "matriarch mama," but not in a stereotyped, bossy, domineering way. Traditionally, a matriarch is a senior member of her clan, one who understands and upholds the values distinct to her family. She provides continuity to her children and grandchildren through her leadership, encouraging them to discover and claim their own places in the family legacy. She pulls lessons of the past into actions for the future, drawing from the roots in order to grow the leaves of the family tree.

From the viewpoint of scripture, she's a combination of the Titus 2 older woman and the Proverbs 31 wife of noble character. A woman of faith, with experience in industry, wisdom, compassion, conscience, and human nature, she desires to share her bountiful knowledge to enhance the lives of those she cares deeply about.

I believe God has uniquely equipped and positioned matriarch mamas to invest in the younger generations in our families and community; to nurture, support, and encourage them to build strong faith-lives of their own. We are the new voice in influencer culture.

Your Audience

The proliferation of social media has changed the concept of influence in the last two decades. Unlike movie stars or sports celebrities hired to endorse consumer products, today's influencers create their own content to attract an audience interested in that specific topic. As their audience grows, influencers have the power to affect the purchasing decisions of that audience by leveraging their knowledge, position, or relationship[9]. They adapt their marketing to the best practices of the digital platforms where their target audience (i.e., their "niche") hangs out.

In addition to wielding purchasing power, influencers also present their opinions, skills, and experiences as a commodity of perceived value for their audience. People who follow influencers take their words to heart, assimilating and using that expertise to make their own lives better. This is where matriarch mamas fit into influencer culture, where our experience, skills, and expertise can bring value to our audience and make their lives better. But unlike social media influencers, we find our audience offline.

As matriarch mamas, we are uniquely positioned to influence our kids, our friends' kids, and the next generation of families who live in our communities. They are our

9 Kristen Bousquet, "What Is an Influencer and How Can I Make Money as One?" *Forbes*, 6 Aug. 2024, https://www.forbes.com/sites/kristenbousquet/article/how-to-become-an-influencer. Accessed 10 Mar. 2025.

audience. Real people, in our real lives. But how do we build a relationship with them, and what, specifically, can we offer?

Research shows that the majority of young adults who engage in intentional faith practices in their personal lives also have strong relationships with other Christians. Many come from a faith background, admire the faith of their parents, and acknowledge influential relationships with other adult believers in their lives[10]. Our taking an interest in them, engaging in, and sharing their lives will feel familiar and welcome.

But what about the young adults who didn't have a Christian upbringing, or other influential adults who invested in them during their formative years? They are also part of our audience. What better way to serve them than to model a sincere life of faith and encourage them to consider it for themselves?

So, how do we present the skills and wisdom gained in our active parenting years in a way that this audience will find valuable? In 2 Timothy 1:5 (NIV), the apostle Paul commends his protege Timothy's "sincere faith," learned from his grandmother Lois and his mother Eunice. How can we, like Lois and Eunice, influence and encourage the next generation as they develop sincere faith of their own?

10 David Kinnaman and Mark Matlock, *Faith for Exiles* (Baker Publishing Group, 2019); "Strong Relationships Within Church Add to Resilient Faith in Young Adults," *Barna*, 26 Aug. 2020, https://www.barna.com/research/relationships-build-resilient-faith. Accessed 11 Apr. 2025.

Your Platform

Even though we are matriarch *mamas*, we cannot take a parental approach when interacting with a younger audience. As we consider what "content" we have to share, we must recognize and respect their autonomy as adults. It's not a case of "mama knows best" but "I want to support you as you create your best."

In addition, our message demands delivery through a more intimate platform than the online digital spaces. Our target audience lives in our real-life sphere of influence, which calls for hands-on marketing. But we can't expect them to come to us. We need to go to them. And like any good social media influencer, that means knowing where our peeps hang out.

A family audience is easiest to find—after all, we know where they live. Keeping in regular contact is an important strategy for investing in relationships. But maybe they live far away, or work hours that make visiting difficult. Call on that matriarch mama creativity to stay in touch. Is there a good time each week for a phone call or a video chat? Use asynchronous technology to text or message; send a brief newsy email or a snail mail care package.

You can also connect with the younger generation within your church or community. Do you have neighbors whose parents or grandparents live far away, or friends with no local family for support? Grow an acquaintance into a friendship by engaging people where they hang out. Volunteer in spaces that put you in proximity to young adults or families: your church's nursery or preschool, the community library, or as an after-school tutor. Get a membership at your neighborhood YMCA, show up and cheer at the Little League game, or chat regularly with the parents watching kids on the playground as you walk your dog in the park.

However you choose to engage your community, take a tip from savvy influencers and don't spam them. Give them something of value each time you make contact—whether it's a ready-made meatloaf for dinner on a busy night, or words of encouragement they can take to heart.

Your Message

In my active parenting years, I often felt unequal to the task of raising children. I second-guessed my parenting style, my discipline methods, and which hills I chose to die on. As the kids got older and smarter, I felt more inexperienced and bewildered. As a matriarch mama-in-training, I was surely flunking every subject. Not the stuff influencer platforms are built on.

Yet, in hindsight, I can identify three areas where my experiences formed and informed the "expertise" I can now offer as a matriarch mama. These are faith, character, and practical living skills.

Faith

As a Christian mother, I prayed for my children to understand and accept Jesus Christ as their savior. For the sake of their eternal lives, they needed their own faith relationship with Christ. I couldn't provide it for them, but I could model it.

The snippets we know from scripture about Timothy, the apostle Paul's "true son in the faith" (1 Timothy 1:2, NIV), reveal him to be a young man with a matriarch mama and grandma who modeled faith to him. We learn that Timothy grew up in Lystra in Asia Minor, and that his mother was Jewish and a believer, but his father was Greek (thus presumably an unbeliever) (Acts 16:1, NIV). Without too much conjecture, we presume that the Holy Scriptures he learned "from infancy" which brought him wisdom to accept salvation through faith in Jesus Christ (2 Timothy 3:15, NIV) were taught by these two women, since Paul says, "I am reminded of your sincere faith, which first lived in your grandmother Lois and in your mother Eunice and, I am persuaded, now lives in you also" (2 Timothy 1:5, NIV). Timothy also must have had exposure to meaningful relationships with non-related adults in his faith community, because other believers in his hometown "thought well of him." (Acts 16:1-2, NIV)

One way matriarch mamas can encourage the younger generation to develop their faith is to live their own faith lives unapologetically. We model discipleship when we routinely and openly talk about our relationship with Jesus, the way we trust God and seek to do his will, and even the struggles we have in persevering when times are difficult. And when we share, we open the door for our audience to share in return, creating community in Christ.

If Jesus is a natural part of our lives, he will be a natural part of our conversations. Therefore, we don't need to downplay our faith when talking with unbelievers either. Good manners will usually prevail in our audience, and they will listen to us, provided we are not sermonizing or bludgeoning them with the Word of God. Asking them if you can pray for a specific need, or simply a general blessing over them, is also a highly effective way to keep Jesus in the conversation. Very few people will refuse an offer of prayer.

Character

"Bye, love you! Don't forget your lunch! Pick nice friends and make good choices!" My sister sent her kids to school with this reminder every day from kindergarten through high school. Eventually, it became a humorous farewell whenever anyone left the house. In truth, the friends we pick and the choices we make are important, for they greatly influence the development of our character—the traits and attributes that become part of our nature.

As believers in a holy God, we are called to be holy like him. To develop a godly character, we try to act like Jesus and make choices that align with our maturing Christlikeness. We actually get the most opportunity to practice godliness as we respond to hardship or adversity in our lives.

Paul imparted this same truth to Timothy. He tells Timothy to train himself to be godly by the way he responds to the inevitable criticism that will come his way. "Don't let anyone look down on you because you are young," Paul writes, "but set an example for the believers in speech, in conduct, in love, in faith and in purity" (1 Timothy 4:12, NIV). In other words, demonstrate what pursuing godliness looks like. Paul also encourages Timothy to read Scripture, preach, and teach according to his gifts, knowing that the congregation will watch and learn from Timothy's growth in godly character (1 Timothy 4:7, 12-16, NIV).

What expertise can matriarch mamas offer for building Christlike character and pursuing godliness? Start by telling your salvation story: share how God shaped your character by revealing his nature to you. Then draw from the roots to feed the leaves. Mine your mental family albums for stories of God's faithfulness, times you trusted his provision, or how he directed your family in making a big decision. Remember what promises he kept, and when he brought calm and peace to a situation fraught with worry or chaos. Like Timothy, your audience might be inspired to pursue their own godliness by observing your growth as you saw God at work in your life.

We can also offer guidance when the younger generation needs discernment to respond to adversity. We practically have a degree in thinking three steps ahead, and in pivoting when God redirects a plan. Through time and study in Scripture, we learned the importance of obeying God as we pray to discern his will. We understand the pervasiveness of sin and can point to the lies the enemy uses to cloud people's judgment or trigger an unhealthy emotional response. Our resume is filled with experience, leaving us well-equipped to be a sounding board for our loved ones as they think through their responses to adversity.

Practical Living

My newlywed daughter brought her favorite flannel pajama bottoms to a recent family gathering at my house. "Mama, can you fix these? I snagged the pocket on a corner of the dresser." We shared a conspiratorial grin as she handed over the garment. It's been common knowledge since middle school Home Ec that she didn't inherit my sewing gene, while I'm a third-generation seamstress who was embroidering at my grandma's knee before my seventh birthday. We gave up the dream of that shared mother/daughter hobby years ago, but I can still bless her by mending her stuff.

Practical living skills are perhaps the easiest "content" to share as matriarch mamas because it's a low-risk proposition to offer to teach someone something we know a lot about. Even if, like my daughter, they never develop proficiency, the time spent together is as valuable as the knowledge shared. But even here we don't need to be certified experts to bring value to our audience; we have intangible skills among the practical that will help us serve the younger generations.

One helpful exercise to pinpoint these intangibles is to ask, "What would I say to my eighteen or twenty-four or thirty-year-old self?" A quick shortlist might include an admonition not to be impatient for "real life" to begin, to trust your own instincts, to know there is recovery from failure, to have a plan for handling money, and never be too proud to seek the counsel of others. And oh, look—now you have things to talk about; or in influencer-speak, content to share with a niche-aged audience.

There's still a place for practicalities, too. The woman in Proverbs 31, while fictitious, nevertheless has a variety of skills to pass along or use for the benefit of others. She cares for her home and her children. She can budget and invest, make decisions, prioritize her tasks, and plan for the future. She is not afraid of hard work, and delights that even her most mundane jobs bring blessings to others. And while not formally teaching any of these skills, she is modeling all of them.

But don't be psyched out by her industry. Instead, consider what I believe are the most important descriptions of her: “She speaks with wisdom, and faithful instruction is on her tongue,” and as “a woman who fears the Lord,” who is “to be praised” (Proverbs 31:26, 30b, NIV). She is most concerned with the spiritual state of those in her sphere of influence.

Just like Lois and Eunice, who set the example for Timothy, instructing him by modeling their authentic faith life, helping him to develop into a spiritually mature follower of Christ.

Just like matriarch mamas, who are equipped by God to invest in our families and community to nurture, support, and encourage them to live strong, faith-filled, character-building, practical lives of their own.

Your Calling, and God’s Grace

Empty nest moms have a new calling as matriarch mamas with a voice in influencer culture. For those not on social media, the idea of being an influencer might be a foreign concept. For those who come from a dysfunctional family, the mantle of matriarch might be one you never thought to wear. And what if you sincerely don’t feel qualified to step into this role? You might think you lack a strong enough faith. Or assume that your character is weak or untested because you have a relatively tame salvation story. Or fear that you don’t have any practical wisdom to offer, or any idea how to convey it. Or that, ultimately, you’ll fail to have an impact, especially on your own family.

I can’t say those fears are unfounded. As we strive for the same increasing Christlikeness we want for our audience, we will misstep. We might pick the wrong friend or make the unwise choice. Our stellar example will go unnoticed, while our spectacular failure will go viral. With each adversity, we have the opportunity to respond in humility and to grow in godliness. You can bet our audience will be watching.

Here's the secret every Christian influencer needs to know: We accept this calling through our obedience, and leave the results to God. He has equipped us to do the work. "Each of you should use whatever gift you have received to serve others, as faithful stewards of God's grace," the apostle Peter writes. "If anyone speaks, they should do so as one who speaks the very words of God. If anyone serves, they should do so with the strength God provides, so that in all things God may be praised through Jesus Christ" (1 Peter 4:10-11, NIV).

When we doubt we can fulfill our calling, Jesus says to us the same words he spoke to Paul, "My grace is sufficient for you, for my power is made perfect in weakness" (2 Corinthians 12:9, NIV). Jesus' influence is relational, intentional, and holistic. Ours can be too. If we are relating intentionally with love, our audience won't reject us if we are not perfect or have all the answers. Because we will be pointing them to Jesus, who is, and does.

Conclusion

Empty nest moms have a lot of new opportunities to choose from as we rediscover the next purpose for our lives. But we don't have to retire from parenting. In claiming our role as matriarch mamas, we embrace a calling and an audience in today's influencer culture. Young adults need mentors, people who will give them perspective and help them see their value. The next generation wants our wisdom and will thrive with our love.

And that is what God is calling us to reclaim in our empty nest years—the ability to put on love and share it with one another.

Next Steps

Reflect on your role as a potential influencer. Use the following questions to think about your audience and what you have to offer.

1. What age group or demographic younger than yourself might you enjoy spending time with?
2. Where would you find them in your town?
3. What do you think they need to know or do to make their lives better?
4. Do you prefer talking with people or doing something together to get to know them better?
5. Did you have a mentor or other adult influence in your life as a young adult? How did that impact you?
6. Are you comfortable talking about your faith to others?

Chapter 5

Who Am I Now?

By Hope Intercedes

"THE KING'S DAUGHTER IS ALL GLORIOUS WITHIN."
PSALM 45:13A (NASB)

Glorious? I was feeling a lot of things, but glorious was not one of them.

Stunned. Confused. Alone.

Even a little abandoned ... by God.

Couldn't God have stopped the tragedy from happening?

But He didn't.

And now our home was empty. The bedrooms were empty. The chairs around the table were empty. Everywhere I looked was empty.

Facing an empty nest wasn't supposed to happen for years to come. Our home was supposed to be full and bustling still. But it wasn't full anymore.

And our home wasn't the only thing. My heart felt empty too. Like an echo of the emptiness surrounding me.

I had always found stability in the sovereignty and goodness of God.

I had always loved the verses in Jeremiah 32.

> *"Ah Lord God! Behold, You Yourself have made the heavens and the earth by Your great power and by Your outstretched arm! Nothing is too difficult for You."* (*vs.* 17, NASB)
>
> *"Behold, I am the Lord, the God of all flesh; is anything too difficult for Me?"* (*vs.* 27, NASB)

My heart automatically answered the rhetorical question. Then, as my eyes looked around at our empty home, I began to question the surety of that answer.

Was He big enough for what I was facing?

Could I trust my Father?

My heart hesitated. What was happening? Was I really not sure if I could trust Him to be big enough? Or was I questioning if He would be big enough *for me*?

Since He made the heavens and the earth, then nothing is too difficult for Him. It was clear to see that He could meet any need the future held, but hanging in my heart was the question of whether He would. Would He be there for *me*?

I was still confident that He was the God who made everything and believed that when He made everything, it was good; very good when He was done.

But everything wasn't good anymore.

My life felt more like a desert than the garden He made originally for Adam and Eve. Did they feel like I did when their life turned upside-down? They had enjoyed sweet, authentic fellowship with Him. But that all changed one day when the serpent entered the picture and started tossing doubt on God's love, provision, and goodness. They not only lost their home, but they also tragically lost the complete trust they had in their relationship with God. The next time they heard God's voice, they did not go towards Him in reliance but away from Him in fear. They hid. Hid their confusion. Hid their shame. Hid their questions.

Like Eve in the garden, the enemy had shown up in my life to toss doubt on God's goodness. I didn't want to listen to the doubt, but my heart was so torn it seemed to seep in through the ragged edges.

I didn't know who I was anymore. And I started questioning who God was, too.

I believed He cared. But wondered if He cared for me. Have you been there? Where can we go with our grieving, questioning hearts?

I entered the empty nest through tragedy. Some of you also may have experienced a premature entrance to this season through the death of a child or even multiple children. Or through divorce and a difficult custody battle. Whatever the tragedy, you were not prepared to be at this stage already. Your perspective and identity have been shaken by a daily reality that you did not see coming.

And even for those of you who knew it was coming, there is no way to prepare for the overwhelmingly prominent void that can lay hold of your home and heart. The daily-ness of the loss of identity and purpose is a reality, whether you know it is coming or it is an abrupt change.

Who are you now? Or maybe, we need to ask: who are you still?

When life is rocked and you need to rebuild, it is foundation time. What is the most important part of who I still am?

Before I met and married my husband, before I became a mom, I joined God's family through Jesus. That is eternal and unchanging. Too many things had changed to put hope in something else that could be undone. I needed an unchanging permanent foundation. *I am still God's daughter.*

But ...

I felt abandoned by God. I wanted to hold on tight and believe He would never leave me or forsake me. But why did I feel alone and forgotten?

How could I rebuild a relationship with my Father? If I were going to put my future and my hope into this relationship, I needed reassurance. Is He really with me? Is His Word trustworthy? Does He really come through on His promises?

I wanted to ask, but was it wrong to question God? Could I take these questions to Him? Could I question the Creator of the universe?! I wasn't sure, but then I found someone who could ... and did! I started my journey in the Psalms. Reading them aloud each day.

David was a man after God's own heart, and yet he asked hard and, at times, grief-filled questions. So David became my guide and mentor as I learned to be honest with my heart struggles and questions by reading a Psalm out loud every day. As I read questions that resonated with my heart, I would repeat those as an audible prayer to get used to saying the words. David's heart cries became my heart cries as I opened my heart to my Heavenly Daddy. The Psalms confirmed over and over that He heard my cries, and amazingly, He even bottled my tears!

Picturing God saving, and maybe even treasuring, my tears brought comfort. And comfort was an important step in reaffirming our relationship. I needed to know God cared about the loss of our children. I needed to know His arms were open. That He grieves with me.

Jesus wept with Mary when her brother Lazarus died. He stopped and mourned the loss with her. This was amazing to me because He stopped *on His way* to the tomb to heal Lazarus and bring him back to life! Jesus didn't tell Mary to dry her eyes and get up to watch what He was about to do. He joined her and grieved with her.

That clarified my thinking. Grief has value. I didn't have to prove I had a right to be sad or to mourn. *Weep with those who weep*, Paul encourages us (Romans 12:15, NASB). Compassion is not to rescue but to join. To focus on where the person is right now ... even if the future has great possibilities.

Jesus went to the tomb and raised Lazarus from the dead *after* He wept with Mary. He did not lead her to the hope for the future until after he stopped to grieve with her.

Jesus cares about how we are right now in this moment. He stops and takes time with us. Hears our hearts. Weeps with us. He doesn't rush us through grief. Even though He knows the great potential before us, He gives us time for our hearts to mourn the brokenness of this life.

I had wrongly thought that believing there was hope meant that we shouldn't mourn. Or if we did mourn, then there was something wrong with our faith. What else was I believing that was a wrong understanding of God's presence and compassion?

I was being drawn into wanting to know Him more and build a closer relationship with my heavenly Father.

As the months passed by, practicing the openness and vulnerability with the Psalms transformed my prayer time. I noticed that even if the Psalm starts with a deep struggle, most of the Psalms end with a confident hope!

I wanted to know and trust God like David did! But how?

David had seen God be faithful in his daily needs. David trusted God to help Him, and God did. Before David stood before Goliath with confidence in God, David ran after a lion and a bear and trusted God to help him protect the sheep. He trusted in little things first (*if a lion and bear can be considered little things*!), allowing his faith to grow in God's strength, ability, and care before he stood before Goliath.

Faith.

> "*Now faith is the assurance of things hoped for, the conviction of things not seen.*" *Hebrews* 11:1 (ESV)

David had come to have faith that God was bigger than anything he was facing. And the conviction that God would always fulfill His promises. When Samuel anointed David as God's choice to become the next king, David had faith that God would keep His promise and bring it to pass, even though it would be years before God would remove the current king, Saul, and put David on the throne. Years that King Saul vacillated between honoring David and trying to kill David!

Yet David's confidence in God fulfilling His promise to make him king remained so strong that even when King Saul was on a rampage to hunt down and kill David, David did not retaliate when he came upon the king sleeping. Even though David's men said God had delivered Saul into his hands to kill him, David honored Saul as God's current anointed king and wouldn't harm Saul to hasten his own rise to the throne. David's faith was a strong conviction in God's promise to bring him to kingship in His timing.

And the Psalms are full of David's faith in God's presence and provision. David wrote often as he marveled at God's creativity and power, and majesty. His eyes were on God, and his heart was devoted to looking to Him. Faith was key to David being able to end most Psalms with hope.

Where had I put my faith? Had I put it in a God who did things the way I expected? I didn't want it to be. I wanted to trust in God's goodness even when things didn't go as I planned or thought they would. I wanted to learn to trust God even when I had hard questions.

Hebrews 11 is filled with people of faith. David gets an honorable mention in this *Hall of Faith* along with other familiar names and amazing events. Men like Abel and Enoch, and Noah.

Moses, another Psalm writer, is mentioned multiple times in the *Hall of Faith*. He saw God do "impossible with man" things because of his faith.

Moses had seen God fulfill multiple judgments on Egypt, and now the death angel was coming. By faith, Moses told the people how to prepare their homes so that the death angel would "Passover" them.

Then, after leaving Egypt, Moses had a big need. The mighty Egyptian army was coming after them. By faith, Moses followed God's instruction, lifted his staff, stretched out his hand, and saw the Red Sea part! God had promised to deliver them, and He would be true to His promise.

Rahab did a small, simple thing with great faith. Trusting God that placing a red cord in the window would protect her family from the destruction that would soon be crashing down around her.

Others also saw God be true to His promises even when they struggled to believe, like Sarah. She had the joy of conception even long past the normal age "*since she counted Him faithful who had promised*" (Hebrews 11:11, ASV).

Having faith that God will do what He says He will do is key in all of the great events of the Bible. God uses those who have faith in His promises. And that is the other key: His promises. Not my ideas. My faith has to be in what God says He will do. Not what I want Him to do.

I wanted my home to be back to "normal." I wanted to go back in time. I was unsure of going forward into the future.

Like me, Abraham was asked to leave the familiar behind to go into an unknown future. Unlike me, he was willing to go wherever God led him. He wasn't given details or a destination. But God was with him.

That reality became key as I saw its prominence throughout His Word: God's presence. I was seeing that I did not need to go into this unknown future alone ... *if* I was willing to place my faith in His promises.

"I will never leave you, nor forsake you."
Hebrews 13:5b (NKJV)

"Do not be afraid, nor be dismayed, for the Lord your God is with you wherever you go." Joshua 1:9b (NKJV)

"Even though I walk through the valley of the shadow of death, I fear no evil, for You are with me."
Psalm 23:4a (NASB)

Faith in His promises began for me by writing promises down as I came across them in my reading time. Then I taped those promises to the insides of my kitchen cupboard doors. When I was overwhelmed or struggling with my grief, I could open a door, read the promise, and be reminded of a solid place to stand.

Was my Father big enough for what I was facing?

He was big enough for David when he faced Goliath. He was big enough for Moses at the Red Sea. He was big enough for Rahab when the Jericho walls came crashing down. He was big enough for Abraham as he faced the unknown future. In each instance, we see God's power as they trusted Him.

The more I wrote down promises, the more I saw God's faithfulness in what I was reading. And the more I started to cling to His promises for me. My trust in His Word was growing strong.

But the trust in His love still tugged at my heart.

I kept reading Romans 8, that nothing can separate us from the love of God. Not death or life or any created thing. I believed it in my mind, but my grieving heart still struggled as I looked around my empty home, until one day, when the reality of Calvary sank in. I was reminded that God's love cannot be measured by our circumstances in a fallen world, but in Jesus' outstretched arms ... at Calvary. 1 John 4:10 (NASB) says, "*In this is love, not that we loved God, but that He loved us and sent His Son ...*" to Calvary. Romans 8:32 (NKJV) says, "*He who did not spare His own Son, but delivered Him up for us all ...*" at Calvary.

Calvary. The exceedingly high price of the gift of Jesus truly is the greatest test of God's love for me. How could I ask for more proof?

With the reminder of Jesus' outstretched arms on the cross, I had to believe that nothing could separate me from the love of God, even if my life wasn't what I thought it would or should be. His love was demonstrated truth.

In spending time in His Word, in talking with Him through prayer, we can embrace these time-tested truths and hold on tight to them. Even when we struggle. Even when we feel broken.

Brokenness is not only a way for doubt to seep in. It is also a place for God's truth to pour in. Truth about His presence. Truth about His power. Truth about His faithfulness. Truth about His love.

The trustworthiness of the things I had come to believe was becoming evident. My Father could be trusted.

> "*You, however, continue in the things you have learned and become convinced of, knowing from whom you have learned them .... All scripture is inspired by God and beneficial for teaching, for rebuke, for correction, for training in righteousness; that the man or woman*

of God may be capable, equipped for every good work."
2 *Timothy* 3:14, 16-17 (NASB)

When transitions overwhelm us, God guides us to what we need in those moments to keep going.

I needed to dig down deep into His Word. I needed to become convinced that God was who He said He was and that I could trust Him and His promises. That everything I needed was found there.

I needed wisdom. James 1:5 tells us that wisdom is available when we ask. I also needed purpose. I didn't know what I was to do next. As I continued reading Scripture, it kept mentioning good works.

2 Timothy 3:17 says that Scripture equips us for every good work. Ephesians 2:10 mentions that we are God's workmanship that He created in Christ Jesus to do good works that He has prepared for us to do. Titus 2:14 encourages us to be zealous for good works.

That He still has a purpose for us seems evident since Scripture says that His Word is to equip us, our uniqueness is by design, good works have been prepared for us, and we are encouraged to be zealous in engaging the good works He brings our way.

But what specifically? How do we know what those good works are? Do you like lists? I love lists! Just give me a list and I'll do it! But maybe *what* is the wrong focus?

Maybe purpose is not about the specifics of *what* we do, but purpose is more about the reason and the *why* that we are doing it.

If we are sure He made us, if we are sure He is with us, if we are sure we can trust Him, if we are sure He said we have good works to do, then anything we do with Him guiding us has purpose. Because our purpose is abiding in Him. To know Him, to love Him, and to partner with Him in sharing His love with others.

It doesn't have to be big or exciting. It can be a cup of cold water. Or a plate of cookies to a neighbor. A smile and a kind word to a cashier. A *thank you* to a cleaning person at a rest stop.

God's love and hope woven into our hearts through His Word can shine a light in the lives around us.

What is He prompting you to do? Do that! Keeping in mind that what you do is not as important as *why* you do it! And your *why* is because the King of Heaven loves you and has placed you here to be His ambassador! As His emissary, you are on a mission with your Father!

As we went through the mundane daily-ness of our lives, no one knew the sorrow we were carrying. I think of that now when we are out and about. We never know what each person God brings our way may be facing, and our kindness could be the balm their heart needs. When we are hurting, it seems counterintuitive to try to uplift someone else. But I found that as God poured His compassion for me into my heart and opened my eyes to the pain of others, it helped lighten my load as I reached out to lighten theirs. I am now on a mission wherever I go, looking for opportunities to represent God's love with smiles and kind words of encouragement for everyone, whether friends or strangers. Our loving words or smile can demonstrate that someone cares when they feel alone or forgotten, giving a seed of hope that our Father can plant in their heart and cause to grow.

We still have an impact to make. We can be about our Father's business in this broken world.

Like me, you may be wondering who you are now. I was no longer a full-time mom. But I could still be a full-time daughter if I wanted to cling to my Father. Like Adam in the garden, God was calling to my heart.

Has God entered your garden? Is He calling to you, "Where are you?" Maybe it's time to answer.

Tell Him where you are. Even if it's a hard place. He is reaching out because He cares about you. Psalm 139 tells us that even before a word is on our tongues, He knows it completely. He doesn't need the information. He wants the relationship. The relationship with you as His daughter.

You can nurture that relationship and get to know your heavenly Father more intimately through His Word. And there you can strengthen your trust and faith in His promises. Promises that include being His child, and nothing separating you from His love.

As His daughter, you can share your heart openly and honestly with Him, the highs and the lows. And as you spend time together, you can ask your Father to guide you in the good works He has prepared for you to walk in each day. Whether big or small, the works you do matter for eternity when you do them with Him. He is the King of Kings! And you are His beloved daughter! Embrace a renewed relationship as the devoted DAUGHTER OF THE KING!

Action Points

- What is today's date? Open to that Psalm and read it out loud. Practice opening your heart to your Abba Daddy.
- Do you see a verse that really gives you hope or perspective? Write it down or print it off and tape it to a prominent place where it can remind and encourage you just when you need it!
- When you are ready, ask Him to prompt you about the good work He still has for you to do. He has an opening for an ambassador in your area!

Chapter 6

The Empty Nest and the Free Seabird

By Amy Duckworth Harrington

"'FOR I KNOW THE PLANS I HAVE FOR YOU,' DECLARES THE LORD, 'PLANS TO PROSPER YOU AND NOT TO HARM YOU, PLANS TO GIVE YOU HOPE AND A FUTURE.'" JEREMIAH 29:11 (NIV)

Five years ago, I stumbled upon a dead bird on the beach during COVID. I identified it as a Northern Gannet. The gannet is a seabird that spends most of its time at sea except when raising its young. It is not often seen on land, so it was new to me. At that point in time, we humans were all flailing about on land, trying to figure out how to live in the pandemic. So, I developed the mantra, "Gannet be Done?" when faced with new challenges. While we hid from the chaos, some of us chose to rediscover or reclaim ourselves. I wrote a picture book manuscript about how a juvenile gannet overcomes fear to do what God made gannets to do. They are meant to fledge or leave the nest, fly, dive, swim, catch fish, and return to land and nest in the next season. It is with this story in mind that I approached my own empty nest experience. I gained the freshman ten during the fledge, but I also gained freedom from fear of writing and publishing my words. I put on a new PFD, a personal flotation device, which I call my purpose for doing, based on what God has planned for me. I grabbed a new PFD, a new purpose for moving forward with my life once my children left the nest. In finding my PFD, I left the nest too and headed out to sea.

When the empty nest loomed on the horizon during the fall of my son's senior year, I asked myself, Gannet be done? Could I prepare myself for the emotions I would feel as my son flexed his feathers and stood at the edge of the college cliff? Could I endure the day of the college drop off, the moment he jumped off the cliff into a new world, while I returned to the solitude of the nest? Finally, would I be able to survive the emptiness of the house and face purposeless days ahead? My purpose, my PFD, was always to be a mom, available for my kids as needed. Could I fearlessly move through the stages of the pre- and post-empty nest without the sadness, loneliness, worry, and the loss of my purpose for doing? What would I do? Could I also be the seabird to fledge and leave the comfort of my own nest, forge ahead by reconnecting with my old self, and put on a new PFD as God has planned?

> "'*For I know the plans I have for you,' declares the* LORD, '*plans to prosper you and not to harm you, plans to give you a future and a hope.*'"
>
> Jeremiah 29:11 (NIV)

I held onto this bible verse, focusing on finding what it would be. I completed my freshman year of the empty nest by reclaiming parts of myself that I once enjoyed. I molted into a version of the free bird I once was. I preferred this free-seabird term rather than an empty nester. I didn't want to think of myself as being left behind. That was too depressing. Over the course of the year, I raised my young and prepared for my own return, proudly wearing my PFD.

I'll share my experience, my strength and my continuing hope to sustain the process as it repeats itself. I was determined not to dive into deep sadness but instead set new goals, write through the experience, and fly as God would have for me to do. I didn't feel the typical empty nesting emotions at first, and as I lay out the events, I decided to start with the moment I experienced the free bird feeling, and then I track with stories about how I got to that moment and soared through it. *Gannet be done*? I asked myself? Yes, I could. HOW did I do it? How did I do that empty nest thing? HOW

- H: I was honest with myself. I did not want to be sad. I skipped being sad at the drop-off. I wanted to be excited.
- O: I was open to listening during the selection and acceptance process and while he was away.
- W: I was willing to let go when the time came and then head to sea with my dreams.

I felt the first true emotional winds of the empty nest slam into me three months *after* the fledge. The empty nest emotions showed up in a way I didn't expect. It hit me like a hurricane, slow and steady with a quiet lull after the eye passes through, then the strongest winds and surge after. In the months that followed the college drop-off, I began writing things down. I didn't want to let go of my mother's PFD, but it wasn't getting used to it as much, so I needed a new purpose for doing. In my extended free time, I explored writing, painting, and photography. It was a surprise phone conversation with my freshman fledgling that set me up for the freedom to pursue my writing on a new level. Our conversation rose and fell like the tides while my need to know the current status of my son's physical and mental well-being overflowed. I expressed my genuine concern, which led to more questions and rough seas. I found myself treading water lightly with my words, jotting a few comments down while standing at the counter. I asked simple and hard questions, and it went like this.

"How is school going?" I asked.

"Fine," he stated with no more information.

"How are your classes?

"They're good."

"Really?"

"Yes," he said.

"OK, are you getting to class?" I asked.

"Yes, Mom. Stop asking. You can see that I am," he said.

"I know, but you know I don't check it regularly."

"Then you know." I could feel frustration flooding into his voice. We had a family phone application that tracked where everyone in the family was at any given time. We put it on our phones when the kids got their driving licenses. I won't debate the advantages and disadvantages of this parenting tool here. It isn't always fair to them or us either. It was still on, but I rarely checked it at this point for either boy because they needed their freedom, and so did I. I didn't want or need to know what was happening. My biggest complaint about the location finder was when they let the battery go to zero. I did check it before I made calls. I didn't want to have it ring in class, but what child today actually answers the phone calls anyway? I pictured myself as the ship captain's wife, pacing the widow's walk, looking to the horizon for a glimpse of a returning ship, but instead, I was listening for a ring from my kids. I wasn't anxiously waiting for them to return home. I just wanted to know that they were safe and showing up to class as promised.

I tried a different tack. To tack is to use the wind to move back and forth. Boats do this, and so do birds.

"Have you seen a doctor yet?" I shifted into a new direction because I knew he had been sick with sinus trouble since September, and it was November.

"I am *fine*, Mom. I'll be alright! If it gets bad, I'll get someone to drive me to urgent care."

"But ..." I didn't get the chance to share my urgent care for him because a sudden gust of wind caught the sail, swinging the boom of the sailboat to knock me overboard.

"Mom, you have got to stop worrying about me. You worrying about me is causing me major anxiety."

I am not a fan of this overused word. We all have levels of anxiety. If there were a speech bubble above my head, it would have said, "That's ridiculous! Of course, I'm going to worry about you, I'm your mother." Then the bubble popped. The words didn't make it to my mouth. Maybe God did that,

I'll never know, but I flinched and paused. I felt the capsize when my soul lurched. I attempted to keep myself upright, but my stomach dropped. I closed my eyes and thought back on all the moments in the past year leading up to this. I never felt this sinking sadness of the empty nest when we dropped him off at school. It happened during the call. I accepted his words internally. HOW could I do that without getting upset? These were his honest feelings, not mine. He was being open with me and willing to share them with me in a kind manner.

Seasickness took over. *I was causing him anxiety.* Not an outside situation, person, place, or thing. It was me. I was disoriented. I stared at the chandelier sparkling on the surface of the ceiling. I chose to come up for air. My head bobbed up to the surface. I took deep breaths and my mind ran through my next choices. I didn't want him to think I was angry. I wasn't. I lay down on the couch in our living room. It served as my raft. It was swaying. I listened to my son's voice as he grew into an adult by sharing his words honestly. I choose to keep my thoughts to myself. I saved them for my captain's log, my personal journal, parts that you are now reading.

I grabbed my PFD. Like I explained earlier, my personal flotation device is my purpose for doing at any given time. My purpose for doing so over the last twenty-one years has been to be the best *available* mother I could be. Memories flooded in as I relived last year. At one point, I wondered if he would choose to apply to college, get in, want to go, or simply sign up for the army. I was trying to be the best parent I could be. I have certainly made mistakes over the last decade when it comes to parenting and being a role model, but I have accepted those mistakes with God's guidance.

"Mom! Are you still there?" I heard him ask.

I resurfaced, lifted my wings, and responded out loud far quicker than it took me to write this in my log or type it up here. I grabbed two letters from the alphabet and kept it simple. "OK," just like I did when he informed me that he had submitted his applications.

I balanced my words carefully and said, "Thank you for telling me how you feel."

I took another breath. "It was unfair to place my worry on you."

He needed to bail me out of my worry because it impacted him. He shouldn't have to worry about me worrying. Worrying is one of those emotions that isn't needed, usually goes unfounded, and clutters our minds. He didn't need it. I didn't need it. Worry grounded both of us. I released the worry, the feelings, and the reality of those emotions. I let it go just as I did at the welcome center on his future college campus.

"Ok." A pregnant pause followed. His voice stalled like the wind. I could hear him thinking. I could feel him growing. It felt like an eternity, but we were only seconds stuck in dead air. Then came the breeze of a sigh, "Thanks." Words matter, each one of them. His response mattered and sent us moving forward.

I looked at my feet at the end of the couch. I imagined the back of the boat where Jesus had sat during a storm. In need of some control, I recalled that bible verse, and I thought of the day we left him at college.

> *"That day, when evening came, he said to his disciples, 'Let us go over to the other side.' Leaving the crowd behind, they took him along, just as he was, in the boat. There were also other boats with him. A furious squall came up, and the waves broke over the boat, so that it was nearly swamped. Jesus was in the stern, sleeping on a cushion. The disciples woke him and said to him, 'Teacher, don't you care if we drown?' He got up, rebuked the wind and said to the waves, 'Quiet! Be still!' Then the wind died down and it was completely calm. He said to his disciples, 'Why are you so afraid? Do you still have no faith?' They were terrified."* Mark 4:35-41 (NIV)

Be still. I heard those words. I felt calm. I had faith. I paused. I was not terrified. He was pulling away. We were calm. I had to trust. I was not alone in this parenting journey. It was calm then, and I changed my course of questioning. Instead of asking closed questions, I asked open-ended ones. I took it to the other side. It was going to be ok. I asked questions about his courses. I asked him what he loved to do at school, and even asked if there were new things he was embracing. He told me about some of his new friends, how he was learning to set up classes for next semester (a good sign he wanted to stay), and attending the various social gatherings. He was even trying new foods. My wings lifted with pride at the simplest of joys he experienced. I let go. I had to bail the worry out of my head and have faith.

In the months that followed that phone call, I spent more time in prayer and meditation. I read more scripture, even got an app, and I began to believe and to trust that what he had learned in his eighteen years would keep him afloat or at least his head above water. The wind had shifted in a good direction between us after that conversation. We were able to circle around each other. I was no longer leading the way. I wasn't at the helm of my kids anymore. We had swapped positions. I was freer to pursue my own purpose for doing, my goals, and dreams. The things I had been doing since the nest emptied were there to move me forward.

Now, let us go back a few months and so you can see that the empty nest journey really began a year prior to that conversation when our son came home and announced that he had applied to a college not on the approved list. Internally, my head exploded like the Fourth of July, and the speech bubble said, "Not a chance!" Externally, I passively replied "OK," like it was no big deal. I got experienced at saying OK, giving myself time to pause and think. I acknowledged it and accepted it, and moved on. I chose to let it go swiftly.

I'll admit from the start that it was selfish for me to give directions to my son with his college applications. I suggested several New England schools that were close to his brother, his grandparents were near the sea. This seabird needed the ocean. I admit I heavily encouraged him to consider these schools. At the last minute, he added a new school. We toured a few colleges up north until he began receiving acceptance letters. I was lulled into a calm feeling of peace as the positive acceptance letters rolled in. When the last-minute add-on to our curated list gave him the aye-aye, I felt that I was losing control of the ship. It felt like a classic Nor'easter minus the college in the northeast. For me, it was more a tale of the three little bears meeting the perfect storm all at once. He chose a school that was too big, too uncomfortably far, four hours west, leaving me with a cold feeling and hot flashes. I was one step closer to the cliff's edge, just like the fledgling gannet.

I had to acknowledge that achievement. He wasn't even sure he wanted to go to college, so at that moment, I had to tread lightly and be careful with my words. I wanted us to stay in the same boat. Secretly, I had no intention for him to attend the school, but God had other plans. When he was accepted to this school. Those two letters O and K proved to be very useful, as were the three letters called my PFD. I put on the PFD then. My Purpose for doing so at the time was to accept the process and to document every experience during this empty nest adventure. This chapter is the product of my PFD. You might hold onto my words to keep afloat during your own

Upon his acceptance, I chose to be excited for him on the spot, and I shared with him my college experience. I honestly shared that my college was NOT my parents' choice. They wanted me to attend an in-state school, but I chose an out-of-state school that was too far away, too large, and too cold, just like he did. They let me go anyway. I loved every minute of college, and maybe he would have the same experience. I left my goldilocks thinking to God. I chose to be genuinely excited for him. I honestly opened my mind to the possibilities. I listened to his reasoning. He wanted to be far away from his current high school. He wanted the on-campus college experience. I knew nothing about the school, so I was willing to check it out. I booked a tour. We took the ride out west.

We approached the admissions center late after our lengthy tour. I enjoyed the tour far more than I was willing to admit. My PFD was to listen. I echoed his enthusiasm and comments. I kept any concerns close to me. When my husband and son walked ahead of me, I half hoped that maybe the office was closed. There were grey skies outside, a squall coming up. Inside, it was dark. A young man greeted us and pulled up the acceptance pages. I sat down on the edge of a cliff, a couch at the back of the room, far from what was happening, because I wanted to be present. I felt this way twice before, once at my own wedding and second at my oldest son's graduation. Someone once told me to sit back and be in the moment. I was never good at that. So, I observed far away from the three men with mixed feelings. Don't get me wrong, I'm not an awful parent. I was THRILLED that he had decided to go to college. Just not this one.

As we left the welcome center, I looked up at the school banners. "Let's Go!" The school motto was everywhere, and I was reminded that my recovery motto is "Let Go—Let God." The young staffer called out and handed my son a small pennant that said, "Let's Go!" I believe that was a true sign. I found my balance again as I watched him fly. I heard our son say, "Let's go!" He was ready to get on the road. Making this course-changing decision had weighed on him. Maybe he was ready to get on the road to life? I could not say. This was a cliff jump into the sea for me, my empty nest experience.

We jumped back in the truck once he made his decision and settled back for the four-hour drive home. I felt numb. We had done it. We jumped back on the college boat for a second time. This one was scary, though. I had to trust. I began praying for him and us that this would work out, but the destination was foggy. I could not see into the future. This human I created left me capsized and treading cold January water. He was choosing to jump from the mothership by going to college. As I looked at him asleep in the back seat, I remembered staring awestruck back at him in his infant car seat seventeen years ago. Isn't this what I hoped for and prepared him to do? Maybe, but this isn't how I planned it, and I am definitely a planner. His decision caused my parenting boat to capsize. I took a deep breath and let it go. God was in the boat with me. I opened the window, letting the wind in. I felt the wind lift my wings to move me forward.

I honestly had an open willingness to keep moving forward, just as the gannet did when it jumped from the cliff. No one gave me advice on how to handle the empty nest fledge, I had to jump off the cliff and figure it out on my own. I had to plan, prepare, and provision for the fledge on my own. In doing so, I provisioned for my own fledge in the form of reclaiming myself. Dictionary.com defines the word provision as "the arrangement or preparation beforehand, as for the doing of something, the meeting of needs, the supplying of means, etc., something provided: a measure or other means for meeting a need." I did everything in my power to plan for the emotions and the physical move from the nest to the college dorm. I did not have as much control as I had hoped, and so I learned to let go.

On the day of drop off, we raised our wings and left the cliff smoothly. I let go and let the wind place him where he needed to be for now. Nothing is permanent, and that gave me comfort. My sails filled with pride. I wasn't sad, I didn't cry during the drop off. It was weird. I rode out the emotions I thought I was supposed to feel after eighteen years of landlocked caregiving. I chose to be happy and excited for him. I grabbed the things I thought he needed that made me feel better. Just ask him about the yellow-topped bin under his bed, and he will tell you it's full of useful stuff, a surprise of treasures each time he opens it, batteries, deodorant, and a toilet wand (that never got used!) I had a good laugh at the flotsam and jetsam in his dorm room when we helped pack him up at the end of the year.

I felt calm as we watched him fledge or walk away while we old seabirds returned to our nesting place. My husband and I were on this new journey, also taking off, but I was the one really being released. These opposing emotions would stay with me during the first year. I rocked, I fear of empty nest, sad feelings, and anticipation for the months before the nest emptied and months after. I stayed upright, though, when I looked back at the empty seat in the truck, and then I looked ahead. I remembered that passage in the bible, where the apostles cried out for Jesus, who was apparently sleeping at the helm, but he wasn't sleeping. He was aware. He calmed the seas. I knew God was here and would be there for me on this next leg of my journey.

This perspective changed everything for me. This free mama seabird (me) had goals and dreams harbored in my soul, waiting. While I am now securely immersed in the empty nest experience, I am grateful it was not filled with many tears, empty hours of wandering with a pervasive fog of sadness. As a stay-at-home mother, I initially thought I would be drowning in grief without the day-to-day routine of caring for the big people I made. I was glad not to be sad because I practiced and provisioned for that leg of the journey. Always thinking of birds, I was reminded of the grebe. They build their nest on the water, lashing it to grasses and reeds. Sometimes, their nests float away after the birds are gone. But we weren't going anywhere. We had the freedom to leave and come back, though.

When my husband and I returned home, it was late. I bobbed around from room to room in the house but avoided his room. For the first three weeks. I shut the door so that it felt as if he were still in there. Months have gone by, and the door is now open. Their tiny bedrooms were like abandoned boat slips waiting for my boys to return. The sunlight reflected off the orange walls in his room. When I opened the doors, the glare cheerily greeted me in the morning like a neon sign. Our dog, Shark Finn, circled me constantly begging for attention, reminding me to take time to walk outside. While I embraced the quiet for some time, I learned to let the loud music play in the house. Jesus had a cushion on the boat, while I have a pillow that says, "Every day is a fresh start." That is how I felt. Every day was a fresh start for me.

I gathered a flock of people to help me on this journey, a few friends who had survived the empty nest, and a few who were experiencing it at the same time as me. I asked people for help, including a mom whose son would be attending with my son in the fall. I asked other parents, including my own parents, for advice, and finally, I reluctantly joined the mountaineer parent Facebook group, and while not a fan of online communities, they help us survive. All together, we were a motley crew of writers, artists, golfers, tennis players, and pickleball dinkers all trying to stay out of the kitchen (the space to avoid on the pickleball court) and away from our fledglings anxious to fly. I had people and sport to balance my life, and a little yoga was helpful too.

Early on during the pre-fledge or drop off, I planned, and I set myself up to be so busy and out of the nest or out to sea as often as possible. Like the Gannet, I only needed to be back at the nest when my young were there. I had been playing a lot of pickleball, so I continued doing that, but I missed playing tennis, so I picked up the tennis racket again. I signed up for a writing course to work on my book tentatively called *Uncapsize-Right Yourself!* I trademarked that phrase just for fun. I took an illustration course so I could create cartoon characters out of my gannet drawings.

I attended two different writing conferences on my own, over seven hours away. As a result of that motivation push, I ghostwrote and published my mother's memoir, and I completed this chapter for a collaboration book. I discovered God's plan for me this season. Really, what I decided was that I wanted to create something from my notes and publish it. What I learned was that his plan was for me to put on a new PFD for my purpose while still balancing my availability as a mother. In the fall, I went to an in-person conference by myself and met with my Pod 13 writing accountability group. We met two years prior at an online conference and met for the first time in person., I learned about what I would need to do to market my book and get noticed, something I am not keen on.

It was very weird for a few weeks. I would stop and think I had forgotten to pick up someone! Those moments of panic soon dissolved like salt in the sea. The salty not being needed thing stung a little, but I rinsed it off while keeping myself busy with writing, painting, and pickleball. I wasn't lonely because I had prepared for this. I started to declutter and bail out the junk in the house. As a former teacher. I have a habit of keeping miscellaneous things that I might need for a lesson plan. I continue to keep things in various drawers. I made it my goal to bail out some of the things that were cluttering up the house, the basement, and the garden. I began clearing out the flotsam drawer and closet, one at a time. It wasn't so difficult, and I felt proud of myself. No one noticed any of it but me. I re-covered the kitchen chairs. I ordered a new window that I can finally see through now. I painted the kick marks under the kitchen counter. That was noticed by one family member. Again, I am not one who likes to be noticed.

In the spring, I attended what I called my PFD conference called Remarkable You. I further immersed myself in the process of reclaiming myself, who I am now, and what I really want to be and do in the future. I was encouraged to dream, plan, do, and review. My dream is to get *Gannet be done?* In print, and yes, I have a plan because yes, it can be done. Of course, there will be plenty of room for review, too, because I have more manuscripts ready to be published in the future.

I accepted the empty nest process fivefold by making choices that involved trying new goals and finishing old ones. I dove into things that were good for me, created a community, wrote regularly, practiced painting, and played pickleball. I joined an online community and flew with a cool flock of people all working towards their personal goals. I buckled up my PFD (purpose for doing), which at the time of that "worry call" was to document the empty nest experience and finish my mother's memoir.

I learned how to paint waves because I loved taking photographs of the waves at the beach and capturing the limelight as it filtered through the waves. I played pickleball at a new place. I jumped back into playing tennis again, adding new crew members to my lifeboat. I am bailing out the junk, turning my tiller of gratitude, and returning safely to my harbor, having learned from my experience and documenting it in my logbook. I balanced time between my home and visiting my parents, who lived near the sea. Back and forth I went. The kids joked that I was never home. I was kind of out to sea, a lot. It was freeing and amazing!

I learned that the nest is never empty, and not because I am constantly moving from it, but because my children still need me wherever I am. They still seek advice, require a resting place outside of the school year, and if I am not mistaken, they like us old birds a little. We genuinely enjoy it when they come home to roost. The most recent advice I heard was that your children *never really leave.* I wish someone had told me that earlier; I might have saved myself some worry. Putting these positive reminders that life is great and God is good in place was my way of provisioning for the empty nest, so I, too, could leave the safety of the harbor and be the free seabird I once was twenty-three years ago! I put my PFD on, jumped, and took flight from my own nest, knowing that Jesus was not asleep at the stern of the boat and that God really had a plan for this old seabird.

I acknowledged that my boys were growing up. My son didn't tell me that he didn't need me anymore. He told me he didn't need me to worry about him out loud. I got that. I did not need to involve myself in everything anymore. I spiritually reached out to him through prayer and meditation. I could do those things. I had to do those things. I could provide advice as needed, money for a haircut, and gas cash for the ride home at winter break. I made myself available. Secretly, I still believe they need us, maybe just knowing we are in their boat to calm the seas as needed is enough. I went into this empty nest experience with a boatload of worry. I will always have that as a mother, but I can manage it. I have learned to uncapsize and transform it into acceptance, joy, a chapter, a book, a painting, a down-the-line pickleball return on the court, by choosing new directions swiftly, gathering my crew, finding balance, decluttering, and bailing out the flotsam and taking flight. My Mom PFD, my purpose for doing so will always be to keep my children safe and be available so they know they can come to me for anything and talk with me. I will always wear this invisible PFD, my "mom" life jacket. I rejoice that my boys and I have a relationship where we do talk honestly as we can with each other. I am still here to model adult behavior to provide for my children's future and my own.

The boys are back in the nest for summer break, and I have a brand new summer PFD. My purpose is to support his continued school and work endeavors and while focusing on finishing Gannet be Done. It has brought me joy to document this year of the empty nest. This next year, I am pledging to photograph, paint, and publish a few picture books. I continue to log my thoughts. Putting these thoughts into this chapter has proven to be the biggest challenge since those "let go of the worry" words back in November were spoken. Now my worry is that my words have not properly conveyed my experience, strength, and hope for you. But that is not up to me, so I will let that go too. I am free to pursue my dreams.

This seabird found her purpose for the year. How did she do it? She was honest with herself, open to listening and learn, and willing to try something old, new, borrowed, or blue. Yes, I just threw that in there to see if you recognized it as something new.

- Playing tennis was something old to me.
- Learning to illustrate was something new for me.
- My mother's memories for her memoir were something borrowed.
- Photographing the blue and the green of the wave was my something blue.

Next Steps

Any one and all together, these actions served as my PFD. Go ahead and define your own PFD, Your Purpose for Doing. Your purpose for right now can be pulled from your past, your present, and your future dreams. Be the seabird and soar towards them. Do what you enjoy doing with the gifts you have been given by God.

"For we are his workmanship, created in Christ Jesus for good works, which God prepared beforehand, that we should walk in them." Ephesians 2:10 (ESV)

Chapter 7

A Three-Year Growth Plan

By Francesca Fallone-Montgomery, OFS

"I CAN DO ALL THINGS THROUGH CHRIST WHO STRENGTHENS ME." PHILIPPIANS 4:13 (NKJV)

For years, I drove my only child back and forth from school. Every time we were on those car rides, we talked, laughed, sang, and prayed together. One morning was different, though. After dropping him off that morning, I went to the nearby church and sat in a pew staring at the crucifix. No prayer, no words, no tears, just emptiness and silence. Then, I heard a voice in my heart: "You are my child; I will not abandon you. He is my child, too; I will not abandon him either!" I felt reassured, but I was still upset. Little did I know that that year was the beginning of a three-year growth plan.

The Year of Discernment

As an Italian who immigrated to the US in my late twenties, my experience has been that Italian kids go to college in the same town where they grew up. They stay in the family home until they have a good job or get married, so letting my son go to college six hours away was an unacceptable reality. I realized that by becoming an American, I had already given up several things about Italy, myself, and my family culture to embrace the one of my husband's family, which was primarily him and his mom. I even wondered if I did the right thing by marrying someone from a different country who did not know me as well as my family, not even after over twenty years together. However, the thought of not being my son's mother gave me chills, and I immediately stopped doubting my choice to marry my husband. After all, he is an incredibly good man, and we do love one another. Being empty nesters might be what we need to nourish our marriage.

That afternoon, when I picked my son up from school for the last time, I asked him if he wanted to go out for ice cream to celebrate. He answered that he had mixed feelings about his imminent departure to college. I reminded him that he chose a college away from home and that I respected his desire to leave town. I also admitted that it was hard for me to let him go, too, but that he had options and that I would back him up no matter what. He then said to me: "I made my decision, but while I am there following my dreams, you should do the same. Promise?" I turned towards him quickly with a smile and said: "Yes, amore. This is going to be a good life chapter for all of us!"

Then, high school graduation night arrived. I put on a smile, but inside I was sad. Students were seated on the football field with their backs to u,s family and friends on the bleachers. At the end of the ceremony, a special song blasted on the high school speakers as all the students threw their caps in the air and spread out all over. It was one of my and my son's favorite songs, so I felt the urge to be near him, but I could not identify where he was in the waves of green gowns. I tried to bravely run toward those waves while recording on my phone, but I could not spot him. Paying attention to the camera angle, I tripped on the bleacher's steps and almost fell. This is where, laughing, I thought about the "dad" in the movie *The Father of the Bride* where after hosting a large wedding gathering at his own house to send off his daughter and new son-in-law to their honeymoon, the father of the bride is getting down the stairs, eyes on the crowed front door trying to catch his daughter's eyes as the newlywed couple was leaving. Unfortunately, the crowd prevented him from making it in time to see her off. The look on his face read "There my baby goes, all grown up, moving forward in life without looking back ... I am just another face in the crowd." Fortunately, my situation was not so dramatic, and as the song was ending, I realized that my husband and my mother-in-law somehow managed to make way toward my son. Finally, I knew which direction to walk on the field.

I reached him as he was starting to walk toward a friend, so I called him, and he turned around, giving me the sweetest smile. I smiled back, but my soul was aching at the thought that in less than three months, I would have to drop him off at college far away from home. On top of that, I was about to turn fifty years old, and I wondered who I was and why this number numbed my enthusiasm. Maybe because my dad had recently passed away, and I did not want to celebrate this milestone without him. Perhaps because I knew that I would be celebrated differently without the opportunity to share a meal, dance, and open gifts with my family of origin. I knew that for them, being far away from me on my big 50th was going to be sad, and it was a painful reminder of the fact that I left my nest. Now I was about to experience the same thing, letting my son move miles away. I prayed and hoped that he would not go as far as to be in a different country, yet I knew this could happen, too. I thought about his love to learn and speak other languages, and the possibility of a study abroad program, and my mind started spinning in a tornado of "worst-case" scenarios.

The next two months were not much better. I was trying to smile and help my son get ready for college life, but in my mind, I dreaded college move-in day. I started questioning the quality of life without my son around the house. Would my husband even notice me, or would he go about his way, having weekly lunch dates with his mother, letting me deal with my crisis on my own? That is when I thought that maybe I did need a solo trip where I could look within and listen to God's whisper in the ocean waves! So, that was my fiftieth birthday gift: Two and a half days at the beach on my own. Up to an hour before leaving the house, I had conflicting thoughts: Should I really go alone? I knew my husband could not take off from work at that time, but should my son need this too, since in just a few weeks he is going to college? However, deep in my heart, I knew that being near the beach on my own was what I needed at that moment to summon my strength before our upcoming family trip to college land.

When I got there, the perky receptionist asked if I was there for a special occasion. I replied: "Not really, I am a writer and need some solo time." He smiled and offered to let them know if there was anything I needed during my stay. My heart jumped as I realized that I had just declared to be a writer, when, if it were not for my son's encouragement, I would not have started the process of publishing my first children's story series. Why did I say that? I dreamed of being an author, but I also used to enjoy singing Jazz. Then Covid hit me twice, and my singing voice was not the same. So, was my subconscious telling me that it was time to use my voice in written words instead of songs?

While all of that was going through my head, I arrived in my room. Wow! The ocean view was breathtaking, so I got closer to the window, and that's when I wanted to scream. I thought to myself: "Really, God? That is a nice sense of humor you have!" Indeed, the first thing I see on the sand is a wooden arch covered with flowers, with a cross in the middle, and a small table covered in a white tablecloth, a couple standing under the arch holding hands, exchanging wedding vows! So, I talked to God in my head: "Are you kidding me, Father? ... I was almost annoyed about finding this. Right outside my otherwise peaceful ocean view.

I was there alone to rediscover and reclaim myself, and now I was reminded that I am a wife, in a marriage that was not what I expected, yet gave me the gift of being a mother. So, I questioned why I was even on this solo trip. That's when I laid on the bed one item for each of the current roles in my life: the wedding band, a picture of my son, a book about discernment, my laptop I had brought for a work Zoom meeting the following morning, a journal representing my writing, my Franciscan Tau cross pendant and my jazz songbook. Then I said a prayer and asked God to lead me. My eyes fell on the book by the title: *Pray, Decide, and Don't Worry*.[11] I bought it for this trip, so I opened it and realized that it was written by a Catholic married couple in collaboration with Fr. Michael Schmitz. So, I took the book with a sigh, opened the balcony door, sat out there, and started reading it. Gradually, the sounds of the wedding celebration below disappeared as the rhythm of the ocean waves took over as a perfect soundtrack to my reading time. The sunset came, and I was still deep in my prayerful reading. Then, as promised, I called my boys back home. We have a beautiful family tradition to pray together in the evening. So, we briefly talked and then prayed together. Saying good night felt weird, though. I had two beds in the room, so I felt even lonelier.

That night, I had a dream in which my husband got up from the bed in the middle of the night to go to the bathroom, and on his way back, he leaned towards me with his eyeglasses on and a big smile. So, I asked him, "How did you get here?" To which he answered, "How did *you* get here"? Then I woke up. I looked at the clock, which read 5:22 (ironically, the date of our marriage). It felt so real that I had to check the bathroom to see if he was there. In my dream, I looked at my husband as a woman in love, and he looked at me with loving eyes, too. I prayed on it and reflected on the possibility that as a couple, we are going to be fine, and we are going to rediscover our love. Still, I was worried about our son. We have such a beautiful relationship, and being his mom has been the primary source of my joy. So, I prayed

11 Jackie Angel, Bobby Angel, and Fr. Mike Schmitz. *Pray, Decide, and Don't Worry: Five Steps to Discerning God's Will*. Ascension Press, 2019.

for him and our family, especially during my two daily walks with God on the shore.

I was missing being at home, but I had to stay and undo one or two more knots in my heart, so I sat on the balcony and continued my inner search through reading and writing time. After that, I wrote some more and realized I might just have identified my calling. I called home for our prayer time and told my boys that I found peace in realizing that I am a child of God, and I want to serve Him and His people with my gifts, though I was not sure yet how to do that. When I mentioned my revelation, my son asked if I had made any progress on my writing project. Indeed, I had finished my first revision of my movie script. My heart leaped, and a question popped in: Could writing be part of my calling? It warmed my heart that my son asked about my writing, as he knew I had almost given up being an author. So, I prayed that he would never give up on his dreams.

The following day, being my last full day there, I decided to take an extra walk, inviting the Holy Spirit to make His presence known to me. It was then that I had an interesting encounter. I was enjoying my Divine walking companion so much that I did not notice the clouds rolling in, and a torrential rain fell on me. Instead of getting upset, I said to myself, "WOW! Ask and you shall receive, uh?" I had just asked the Lord to cleanse my heart and mind of anything negative that would prevent me from being in tune with His plan for me. So, I started running with the biggest smile on my face and that's when I encountered this sweet lady, old enough to be my mother, who calmly walking in the rain said to me: "Are you enjoying yourself?" and all I could say was, “Yes, in the cleansing water from Heaven!” She then disappeared.

That evening at sunset, I was thinking about Mary, how she had to let her son go and complete His divine mission on a cross, and how she had the most amazing privilege of being Jesus’s mom, even knowing that He is the son of God, only entrusted to her while on earth. I imagined how she must have been lovingly and respectfully at his side, always acknowledging him as the Son of God first and foremost. So, I asked her to be at my son’s side too. That night, during my sunset walk, I saw a few people gathered on the shore, all pointing at something in the water. There were two beautiful dolphins, one a little bigger than the other, leaping in and out of the water. It was amazing, and I immediately thought about a parent and a child leaping together through life, yet not holding hands or fins. I felt such peace as I realized that Mary had to let go, and all mothers and all animals go through this letting go of their little ones as they grow. I knew then that she and the Holy Spirit were reassuring me that my son would never be alone. Even when I let go of him geographically. More so, I knew that God does not let any of His children take big leaps on their own. He is always with us, no matter what. So, with Him in my heart, I could face dropping my son off at college because that is not the end of my being his mom, simply the beginning of a different way to be his mother.

When I got home, I gave my son a fridge magnet with two dolphins on it and told him about this beautiful experience. I got a hug and a smile. He then said he wanted to get a cross to wear around his neck. I know I am an Italian

Catholic mom, yet I have not given my son a cross pendant yet. What is wrong with me? I kiddingly thought with the voice of Al Pacino in my head saying: 'This is an offer I cannot refuse!" Once in a local Christian store, we both were drawn to the same cross among others on the display. It had a quote engraved on it: "I can do all things through Christ who strengthens me." (Philippians 4:13, NKJV) He chose it on the spot with a smile. This was the one for him with a great message for both of us.

The Year of Challenges

When freshman year started, dropping off my son at college was like cutting my heart in two with a hot knife. I know I sound dramatic, but some of you may have experienced this too. Also, when we had our college tour, we saw a college dorm room that was top of the line, remodeled, and spacious with a short half wall dividing the two roommates' areas. However, when our son got into his assigned room, it was big enough for only one student, but he and his roommate had to share it, and the guy had already moved in, choosing the larger side of the room. I asked my son if he wanted to talk to someone about changing rooms, but his answer was humbling and warm. He said, "If this is where God wants me to be for now, this is where I need to be." So, after we spent a week in a nearby hotel, we had to leave him where, apparently, God needed him to be, but none of us really wanted him to stay. We left, promising to be back to visit soon.

Once back home, I felt closer to my husband, united by the unbearable pain of missing our son around the house. We grew stronger by continuing to pray together with him every night through WhatsApp. Still, that first semester was tough on all of us. Our son's efforts to adjust were handled with grace and maturity, which inspired us and made an impact on his roommate as well. However, during Christmas break, our son changed his major and realized he needed to transfer to a different college with a better program for him. Since it was in the middle of the academic year, the transfer included a viable option to finish the year online, so he did. It was during that spring semester at home that he realized that he still wanted to go out of town to the university he could transfer to in the fall. It could have been a setback, but when you make decisions in prayer, God has a way to make things work in your best interest.

Having our son at home that semester was a Godsend for all of us since his grandmother unexpectedly ended up in the hospital, suffered a stroke, and passed away. A week after my mother-in-law died, we also lost my son's godmother, the wonderful wife of our best friend and best man at our wedding. Being together as a family during those months was a strengthening experience for all of us. Also, my beloved mother-in-law, lying in the hospital between heaven and earth, unable to move 95 % of her body, gave us all a special message in a dream. Our niece, who lives in Europe but knew her well and even called her Noni, dreamed that she saw her happily dancing, and so asked Noni how that was possible since she was paralyzed, and that is when my mother-in-law responded: "What is visible is not what matters!" This message gave us such courage to accept the fact that Noni was not going to overcome this, and we had to let her go, too. It was a very difficult time for my husband, especially, and for my son naturally, but for me too, because thanks to God, she and I had worked on our relationship to the point of feeling like a mother and a daughter. However, through the beautiful message she gave our niece, we were all reminded that the geographic distance does not matter, the inability to be in the same room does not destroy the love that we share because our spirits are connected.

The Year of Determination

Here we were again, but this time we were all better prepared. After this second college move-in day, entering a quiet house a few months after those losses, somehow, was not as bad, knowing that with our deep spiritual connection, we are "there" for one another always. So, with that reminder in our hearts, we faced our son's sophomore year, the first full academic year without him in the house. We were experiencing the Philippians 4:13 verse, and we were embracing its message with determination.

Sadly, since my mother-in-law and our dear friend died. We lost two more family members and three other dear friends, including my manager at the bookstore where I worked, and my Franciscan sponsor, who was like a mother figure to me. In addition, in the fall, I had two health scares and a couple of biopsies, thankfully with good results. In the spring, my husband, who had undergone a seven-bypass surgery over a decade before, had an unexpected heart procedure. Sitting alone in the waiting room with our son miles away and no other family in town, I prayed for strength and healing. I needed my husband to be well. Thankfully, all went even better than hoped, and I was able to bring him home the following morning. However, that evening, as I was praying in church, I got a short call from our son, who was in a car accident near his college, and told me that the car was gone. Then he said, "They are coming, I've got to go," and hung up as I was telling him to pray and stay calm.

"Is this how it feels to faint?" I wondered. I knelt and prayed. A sweet lady who happened to be there when I got the call prayed with me. Then we both realized I needed to go home to wait for the call. The piercing sound of the ambulance and his scared voice were still ringing in my ears throughout my ride back home, then there was silence. That silence was so loud that I thought even my heartbeat had stopped. It felt like God overestimated my strength this time, as I knew I could not handle more bad news. I needed good news, and I needed it now! That hour was the longest of my life. My husband and I were pacing the floor and praying, determined to believe in Philippians 4:13. Finally, our son called back. He was ok. The morning after, we drove to see him. Indeed, he was miraculously physically fine, and we were able to stay near his college for a week, making sure we were all well enough to get back to our normal routines.

When spring break came, it was a true joy to have him home, and we knew that we could go through the remainder of the semester stronger than before. We made plans for a study abroad, an internship, and his remaining academic journey. We all got through it, but without our faith, we could not have handled any of this. Praying every night together, relying on God's help daily, trusting in Him, and asking the Holy Spirit to be our guide every day in every decision has proven to be a way to strengthen our faith and grow even closer as a family, both emotionally and spiritually. Indeed, we can face and do anything through Him who gives us strength.

Lessons from the Growth Plan

Over these three years, I learned that fear can be an emotional derailment of our personal growth tracks. The anticipation of an imaginary worst-case scenario blinded me from the graces of the journey and the light of Christ's presence in it. Inviting the Holy Spirit into our lives and striving to cooperate with Him are indeed strengthening sources of energy and inner drive. Through Christ, we can indeed do all things, including discern the plan, overcome its challenges, and be determined to implement His growth plan for us. As my husband was learning to live without his mother physically on earth, and our son was learning how to fly solo, my calling to serve God and others got louder. The first people I am learning to serve better are indeed my husband, my son, and our family members, but I am also striving to help others, nourishing my relationship with Christ, to feel His presence and guidance daily. Writing is now part of my service, such as a periodic reflection article for my Franciscan fraternity newsletter, more writing projects in the making, and this awesome book you are reading right now. I also trained to be a faith-based life coach, which led me to start a podcast in the hope of soothing others as they implement their growth plans. I might even resume singing in church, and who knows what other amazing plans God has designed for me!

This has been God's three-year growth plan for us, which did not always make us want to say, "Nice doing business with you" but returned some valuable interests such as these realizations: We may have different relationships and roles in our life, but they are all part of who we are for the rest of our life. We never stop being a child, a parent, a spouse, a family member, a friend, and/or whatever other roles you might have in life, because we are all evolving to be our highest version of ourselves. Every leap, flight, path, and step we might take in life brings us closer to what God's designed plan is. So, the sound of silence of your empty nest does not mean the end of your being a parent, but rather an opportunity to be an even better version of yourself, to embrace a new way to relate to your child or children. Think about the pride you felt when seeing your child walk on his or her own for the first time, and the times that he or she has learned to take care of personal hygiene, and the strength of his/her body. Remember the times that you saw your child manage things on his or her own, after having you as an example of how to manage those things. Your role as a parent mattered then and still does now! Ponder on the rewarding feeling that both you and your child feel when looking back at all that you have overcome together and individually.

I remember leaving Italy and slowly overcoming the challenges of moving to a foreign country and missing my parents, family, and friends. I felt alone yet blessed to have a bridge in my heart that always allows me to reach my loved ones no matter where they are. This bridge is built on Faith, Hope, Love, and the Joy of being loved by God. His love is the bridge that connects all temporal or geographic distances. He is the connection between me and all the people I love. He is the one who created me for the main purpose of loving Him and others, seeking Christ within, and bringing Him to others. Every day is an opportunity to show love for Him as the Father He is.

I often imagine God's loving fatherly eyes watching over me. He knows all that I think and feel. He knows my soul very well, and what is best for me, yet He lets me fail, fall, get back up, and finally succeed. The amazing thing is that He does the same for my husband, for my son, for all my family and friends, the people I know, my fellow writers, and yes, for all of you readers too. He loves all His children! I used to worry about what other people would think or say about my life decisions until I realized that the only one whose opinion I should care about is our Heavenly Father. He is indeed the best parent to all of us. We are all His children, so our kids are simply entrusted to us while we are on earth. But first and foremost, they are part of the same family that we will reunite with in Heaven one day, together in spirit, all as siblings with the same awesome Parent. His superlative parenting skills include endless love and mercy as He prepares for each one of us a place in His wonderful nest! How blessed we truly are!

Your Turn to Start Planning

Now, I want to encourage you to take time to appreciate who you are: A child of God! As such, you are not facing life alone. He is with you always! He has an amazing plan for you that does not end until He calls you Home. So, consider this: Think about your empty nest as an opportunity to take your wings for a spin towards what God calls you to do every day. A nest is always a safe place to land, and your kids will land there again eventually, even after they build a nest of their own. However, the beauty of calling it a nest is to realize that you have wings too. Your spirit needs to soar, just like you taught your kids how to do, and did yourself when you left your own home of origin.

Next, I would like you to sit down and take a couple of deep breaths. Then, close your eyes and feel your essence, get in tune with your heart, and find God in it. If you do not believe in God, do this anyway, reach within, then rest there for a few minutes before coming back to this page.

Welcome back! Now, ask God where He would help you soar today if you let Him. Maybe there is an area of your life, an interest that you have put aside for a while. Think about it for a moment: What brings you joy? What makes you feel fulfilled? Could it be time alone with nature? Could it be using your talents that you ignored while being a busy parent?

Write down your thoughts and pray over them. If you do not pray, just ponder how to act on these thoughts.

Lastly, remember this: You are a wonderful creation of God! Believe it or not, you are uniquely and wonderfully made. So, spread your wings and soar to the highest version of yourself. You will be pleasantly surprised by the view from up there, and you will find God, the Father, at your side, cheering you on!

Chapter 8

Becoming Whole Again: Welcoming God During the Season of Life I Needed Him Most

By Michelle Castro-Proud

"WHEN I AM AFRAID, I PUT MY TRUST IN YOU." PSALM 56:3 (NIV)

WITHOUT GOD

"HE HEALS THE BROKENHEARTED AND BINDS UP THEIR WOUNDS." PSALM 147:3 (NIV)

The day my world turned upside down began at John Wayne Airport. Driving to the airport was normally fun, filled with excitement and anticipation for a vacation. Still, this drive was filled with something very different: feelings of anxiousness, dread, sadness, and the complete unknown. I was dropping off my daughter to fly back east to start her college years. I tried hard to keep a stiff upper lip and be positive, but I'm pretty sure my body language and face showed something very different.

I was arriving as a single mom with my one and only daughter, Ashlee, and would be leaving as an empty nester, all alone. And when I say all alone, I truly felt alone. At this point in my life, I didn't have much of a relationship with God. It was an on-the-surface relationship where I prayed for my daughter, for loved ones, and on rare occasions when I had a need or want. We would go to church on Sundays if we had time, but that was pretty much the extent of it. He knew me completely, but I only knew Him from afar.

My daughter truly was my one and only, and everything I did was in hopes of her being the exact opposite of me. I wanted her to always feel loved, be self-confident, self-sufficient, and never feel like somebody was more important to me than she was. She was amazing to me in every way and was exactly the girl I had prayed for. I was an only child, raising the same, and it was important to me that this child of mine would never feel alone, as I often did. I would always be by her side, and I would be the one she would lean on for all things, or so I thought. Little did I know that day at the airport that it would not be me who would always be by her side. The Lord was the one who would fulfill her needs and always be with her. And He would save me, too. We would both meet Him intimately.

Ashlee grew up being told she was going to go away to college, be successful, and have a wonderful life. But my definition of "going away" meant she would go to a college or university somewhere here in California, and hopefully not more than a couple of hours away. My life revolved around being her mom. When she was born, it was the best day of my life, and I had this little best friend who I loved more than life itself. When her dad and I divorced a few years later, I immersed myself into being Ashlee's mom, doing all things for her and immersing myself in all of her activities – gymnastics, Brownies, and dance class, to name a few. We were busy from morning to night most of the time, and those eighteen years flew by. I can honestly say I never thought about what I was going to do when she went away to college and started her own life. I had not taken the time to think about my future or even define myself. In my head, I was Ashlee's mom, and that was more than enough. I had no idea who I was and what my likes were, or even why I existed.

The summer after Ashlee graduated from high school was spent getting her ready to go away to college, a couple of hours away from home—the perfect scenario I had hoped for. We went to freshmen orientation and spent the night in the dorms a few weeks before she was to move in. But that night she dropped a bombshell. She had changed her mind. She was going back east to college, and she would be leaving in a couple of weeks. I was blindsided. But I supported her in her decision as I usually did, whether I thought it was alright or not. We quickly told the family and, over the next two weeks, got her ready to go. I barely had time to think about what life was going to be like living alone, and with her being so far away. But then it finally hit me: Ashlee's life was just beginning, and I felt like my life, of being her mom, was ending. Who would I even be anymore?

The drive to the airport was filled with silence and tension. After all the packing and rushing to change plans, it was the first time we were sitting quietly together, and suddenly I was able to think about the impact of her quick change in college plans, the emotions of letting her go, and the way it was going to change our lives. I could feel the tears welling up, and the panic arising, but I just wanted to get her there without a scene. As soon as I checked her in at the airport, hugged her goodbye, and told her how proud I was of her and how much I loved her, I walked a few steps and grabbed onto a nearby pillar because I was completely falling apart. Sobs racked my body. I bent over in physical pain, and my heart literally felt like it was broken. I needed a few moments to pull myself together enough to pull myself together enough to go out and find my cart. Then I returned to my house that day, a shell of a person.

For the next few months, I could barely function. It took all my energy to just get to work and then home to do absolutely nothing. I was in a deep depression and did not care about anything. I was a mess in just about every way. I had no desire to laugh, smile, or do anything for myself. Needless to say, I was not handling being alone well at all. None of my friends were going through this, and I felt like none of them could relate. So I went deeper and deeper into my own thoughts and isolation.

After a few months, I started feeling somewhat like myself again. I was still sad and missing Ashlee like crazy, but I became a functioning human and was able to smile here and there. Ashlee came home to visit, and I was so happy to have her home. And, once home, she proceeded to tell me that she was not going back. She was moving back home and going to a local college. I would like to say I jumped for joy, but my reaction surprised me. I was still upset. Maybe I was just still raw. Maybe I was on alert. Maybe I was upset with myself that I had wallowed in my sadness for all that time and wondered why we had to go through that at all. Later, I would find out the answer.

Meeting God

> *"He says, 'Be still, and know that I am God.'"*
>
> Psalm 46:10 (NIV)

Ashlee had been home for a little over a year, and life was good. She was going to college, and I was working and being her mom. The immersing of myself into her life had subsided quite a bit, and I was at a point of slowly rediscovering who I was and what my likes and needs were. It was a very different place to be, but even though I told myself I was content in the place I was in my life, it still felt like something was missing. The lonely feeling was not nearly as intense as when Ashlee was back east, but it was definitely there, and I was trying to ignore it. Looking back now, I see that I had always thought of us as one, as a team, as "we," but had learned that we were not one. We were individuals, both trying to find out who we were separately. We would always be mother and daughter, but we were first and foremost Michelle and Ashlee.

I have never been one who can read between the lines. It takes directness for me to get the gist of something; it needs to be right in my face, where I cannot pretend or run away from the situation. God created me and knew me deeply. He was going to have to show up in a way that I could not deny Him or look the other way and act like I did not see Him. He was going to make me stop with all the chaos and busyness I had created in my life and see that He was right there at every step of my life.

One afternoon, Ashlee came home and told me she had a friend from high school who had turned his life around after he started going to church. She was very curious as to how he was impacted so much by going to this particular church. She and her friend were planning on going on Sunday. I was a little leery about it and asked if I could go with them as well. I was very cautious and was concerned that it was a cult of some sort. I clearly was still a hovering mom.

Sunday arrived, and we went to this small church that looked nothing like the churches I had ever been to in the past. When walking in, something felt different. There was an air in there that felt like someone was breathing life into me—I immediately felt peace. At the time, I didn't know what it was, but I immediately felt what I thought was an "off" feeling and at the same time a sense of calmness. Everybody was so welcoming and kind, but I was still in the mindset that they had ulterior motives. I was apprehensive yet tried to be open-minded at the same time. I was not there to join this church and change my life—I was just there to watch over Ashlee. My thought was that God didn't need or want me. I was a flawed human who was just trying to get by.

Service began, and almost immediately, the worship got to me—my heart, mind, and soul. I felt feelings I had never felt before. I cried and cried and had a really hard time staying in control. I was embarrassed and didn't know what to do but also could not deny the emotions I was having. The pastor preached, and it felt like he was speaking to me directly, like this was meant for my ears only. I questioned in my head if somebody here knew me, knew my past, and knew my struggles. The words being spoken were as if somebody there knew my story. I stopped overthinking and just listened, but as I listened, I became fully aware that nobody in that sanctuary knew my story. It was actually God who knew me and was trying to get my attention, and He most certainly did! So many thoughts went through my mind during that morning as I sat there. Service ended, and now looking back, I walked out of that church a different person than when I arrived. My eyes were opened, and for the first time in a very long time, I had hope.

God showed Himself to me in a way that there was no way I could deny His presence. Although I could not see a physical being, there was no doubt in my mind that He was very real. Many questions were going through my mind as we walked to the car.

Would God love me the way He loved others?

Was I worthy of His love?

Would I be forgiven of all my sins?

Why now, when I'm forty-one years old and do not like change?

True to His promises, He showed Himself very clearly to me over the next few months, and eventually all my questions were answered. I was so used to living a life filled with chaos, insecurities, loneliness, and being unsure of where my life was going to go. Many times, the chaos was in my own mind, and now I didn't want or need to live in that anymore. Living a life of peace and not feeling alone anymore was something I never thought could happen. Peace was what I craved, and the Lord was showing me that He was the only one who could give me that. For the chaos was now exactly what I didn't want in my life. Being still was now all I wanted. In those still moments, I heard from the Lord so clearly, and I longed for those still moments.

God created me and knew me better than anyone else. I became who He intended me to be – not just Ashlee's mom, but a whole being who loved the Lord completely. I had always been one who portrayed that there was joy in my life. I wore a mask that I took off only in the safe place of my home. Now I didn't have to wear the mask anymore. Having God in my life gave me the freedom to be happy, joyous, and filled with love. I had never felt so free in my life. I felt like I had had open heart surgery and had received a new heart.

At the same time that I was beginning my relationship with the Lord, Ashlee was doing the same. We had different journeys, but God was taking our mother-daughter relationship to a deeper place. Life couldn't get any better than this. I was dealing with my past, my shame, and my insecurities. He made sure I knew I truly was forgiven, and I did not feel judged anymore. It was a process and did not happen overnight, but I was not going to give up and let my fear of being alone get the best of me. I was different now: I looked different, and I was loving every minute of my life. No matter where my life took me or what I was feeling, God had been by my side every step of the way. From this point on, I knew I was blessed and thanked Him every day. There were still struggles and many storms came my way, but each time, God has been right by my side. Without Him, every step I took when there was a problem felt so heavy. Now the heaviness is lighter because He carries me through the storms, and He is my safe place, He loves me unconditionally, and He shows me that.

With God

> *"So do not fear, for I am with you; do not be dismayed, for I am your God. I will strengthen you and help you; I will uphold you with my righteous right hand."*
> Isaiah 41:10 (NIV)

A few years later, Ashlee announced she was getting married. As if being thrown into the role of empty nester once was not trying enough, here I was faced with the same challenge of being an empty nester again. How would I fare this time around? This could either make or break me, and I was determined that the latter was not going to be the choice I made this time. I was being given a second chance at something I had failed at terribly years before. This was a very different chapter; one I did not expect or know if I could even endure. One thing was for sure—this time, I would not be facing it alone. God would be by my side every step of the way, and that was my saving grace. Here was my chance to redeem myself. This could be the beginning of me finally choosing peace, grace for myself, and letting go without feeling like I could not survive. This would be the beginning of the next chapter of my life, and I wanted to embrace whatever plans God had for me.

Several months after the wedding, Ashlee and her new husband, Jeremy, asked me to lunch after church one Sunday. I did not think much of the invite and thought it was going to be just a lovely afternoon with the two of them.

Little did I know that my world was about to change again. We sat down to eat, and before I knew it, Ashlee was saying, "Mom, I need to tell you something." As history had shown in our mother-daughter relationship, those seven words were never good news, at least not from my perspective. I could feel my body tightening up and bracing myself for bad news. Even though I had more peace in my life and a relationship with the Lord, at times I still had that old, familiar feeling of fear in me. The mind that would stop me in my tracks and forget who I was. She proceeded to tell me she had received a job offer in Northern California, almost 500 miles away. She was almost done with grad school, and this would be a dream position in her field, which was amazing.

I took a deep breath. Surprising not only myself, but Ashlee and her husband as well, I did not fall apart. I knew this was an offer she could not refuse and that she needed to do what made her happy. This would be the beginning of the self-sufficient, wonderful life I had always wanted for her and had I prayed to God for. I let her know I was so proud of her and hugged her. It was time for Ashlee to live her life and for me to live mine in a healthy, godly manner. Not to say that I was jumping for joy, though; while I was proud and happy for her, I knew my heart was going to break. I adjusted my napkin and tried my best to stay positive and smile. I may have been stoic on the outside, but I was quickly processing the news and was feeling quite nervous on the inside.

In my mind, I imagined we would have the rest of spring and summer together, and they would be moving before the fall, when her new job was to begin. This would give us plenty of time to adjust to the change, and time for me to accept what was happening.

But before I could take the first bite of my lunch, she dropped the next bombshell. They would be moving very soon, probably in a couple of months. I sat up straighter and tried to stay positive. Although I wanted to burst into tears, I also knew that God was right there with me. I am pretty sure that His arms were wrapped around me as we sat outdoors eating our meal. And, boy, did I need His support. I felt like He had prepared me for this moment. Old me would not have been nearly as understanding or calm. I was even surprised that I was seemingly okay. I was not going to be alone this time around. I had God by my side, and He was never going to leave me—that I knew for sure. I was now a different person. I knew what I liked to do, who I was, and I was surrounded by an abundance of love with my family and friends. It was time to get down to business and be there for Ashlee. I let her know that I would do whatever she needed, such as help her pack and/or move.

Here I was in a completely different mindset than the first time Ashlee had moved out. I would like to say that my heart was not breaking and that all was wonderful, but the same feelings of fear and being alone were there. They were more controlled emotions, but nevertheless, I was still a mom losing her child. God knew differently, though; His promises are filled with hope and joy. I prayed for Him to help me stay focused on what good may come out of this situation. I prayed a lot and leaned on my friends and family as well. God truly protected my mind and heart. I had to trust Him or I wouldn't get through it.

Over the next few weeks, Ashlee was so looking forward to her new life up north, which really helped me be okay with her move. I was not scared for her or myself this time around. Having God in my life changed my attitude and even how my body reacted to this situation. On the big moving day, I took the day off work and helped them pack their things. Emotionally, I was able to stay intact and not lose my mind. In fact, I was quite surprised and happy for her. There was no woe in me that day. This was about Ashlee starting her next chapter of life, and I was looking forward to seeing where the Lord would lead her. We said our goodbyes, and I watched them drive off. There were tears that day, but they were tears of joy sprinkled in with the tears of missing her.

There were still challenges, but it didn't feel like I wouldn't survive living alone and having my own life. Ashlee was going to be just fine, and so was I—not alone, but with God. He gave me the strength to carry on and look forward to all the blessings that were going to come for all of us. I traveled to visit as much as I could, all the while believing that they would eventually be moving back to Southern California. God had a different plan, though—a much greater plan than I had ever imagined. I became a grandma to three amazing grandsons in the span of six years. I had no idea that three little boys would fill my heart the way they have. It hasn't always been easy with us not living near each other, but we sure have made the best of the situation. When I hear my grandsons call me Mimi and see the big smiles on their sweet faces, I thank God for all He has done. Everything that I have gone through brought me here. I went from believing that when Ashlee moved out, I was going to be alone forever to knowing that I will never be alone again. God answered my prayers and then some. I know that trials and tribulations will still come, but not without Him guiding me. I will always look back on that day we walked into that unconventional little church as one of the best days of my life!

Things I Learned On My Journey

- You are not alone when you have God in your life—let Him into your heart. Allow Him to make you feel whole in the times when you feel broken, like when your child separates from you or moves out of your home.
- Remember who you were before you were a mom, and tap into those interests, hobbies, and friends again. Fill your life with these possibly forgotten activities.
- If you never thought of your future beyond raising your child. Take some time to envision your future. You have a lifetime ahead of you with a new, fun relationship with your adult child.

Chapter 9

Letting Go: Trusting God Through a Hard Season in Life

By Melissa Lindsey

"IN THEIR HEARTS HUMANS PLAN THEIR COURSE, BUT THE LORD ESTABLISHES THEIR STEPS." PROVERBS 16:9 (NIV)

I woke up on Saturday morning, contorted like a pretzel, with my lower back in knots—all thanks to the little furball snuggling too close. I shifted carefully, but not carefully enough. Caesar, our lovable fourteen-year-old Westie, rotated in circles before flopping onto the bed and snuggling closer to me. With his signature "humph" noise, he silently communicated his intent for another hour of undisturbed sleep before we started the day.

My husband, Jamie, snored softly beside us. The slow pace of a Saturday morning tempted me to drift back to sleep with them, but my mind knew I should stay awake and relish these moments before they ended.

Caesar's age was catching up to him. He was struggling with dementia and neuropathy in his left hind paw. We had been dealing with this for over eight months, and it was progressively getting worse.

The symptoms of dementia began around 5:00 most afternoons. Just like humans, dogs experience what is known as "sundowners." We would know we had lost him again when the blank look would come over his face, and he began to do odd things, like lick the furniture. Licking the furniture is a symptom of doggie dementia ... who knew? It also caused him to get up and wander around in the middle of the night. We were beginning to feel like parents of a newborn instead of the empty nesters we were at this stage in life. Tired didn't even begin to describe it.

To make matters worse, the neuropathy in his paw caused him to bite it repeatedly. It had to be cleaned and bandaged twice daily to prevent him from chewing it off, which was exhausting, too.

Life had been challenging the last few years. My dad passed away during the COVID-19 pandemic, preventing us from being with him in the nursing home when he died. My mom battled cancer, and one of our children had endured suffering in her marriage that no one should ever experience in their entire lives.

Both kids were now hundreds of miles away, leading successful lives, and while I was happy that we had raised two self-sufficient young adults, this was not how I had envisioned life at this stage. While I never wanted to hold my children back, I still missed them something fierce. Without realizing it, Caesar had become our escape. His lively personality had once kept us entertained, and now his health issues kept us busy but also tied down. We were becoming disconnected and complete recluses. We struggled to go anywhere together. If we did, it required planning. We needed someone willing to sit with Caesar, and to arrange this was challenging. On his bad days, he had started biting and could be quite aggressive if you didn't know how to deal with him. As a result, it was just easier to stay home. Jamie was out during the day for work, but I worked from home and grew increasingly depressed.

I tried hard to remain positive, but just when I felt my head was above the surface, something else would drag me under. My company was in a growth stage, and while that was a good problem to have, my work schedule was overwhelming. Due to busyness, taking care of Caesar, and my depressed state, I had cut myself off from most of the world, except for Jamie, and then, on top of everything else, I developed a hormone imbalance. It felt like the perfect storm. I hit a wall.

I cried every single day. I felt unappreciated, and it seemed like life would never be happy again. I began to resent Jamie. He would come home from work and immediately leave to take Caesar for his daily ride. He would be gone for an hour or two, talking to a good friend who lives in our neighborhood. Looking back on it, I can't blame him. I had become a version of myself that even I did not like.

My wake-up call came early one morning when I went out for a walk. I ran into our neighbor, and I was in a mood. I was angry because Jamie spent so much time with him while I wanted him home. The words that came out of my mouth were both judgmental and unkind. As I walked home, I could not believe what I had just done. This was a dear Christian friend who would do anything in the world for us. How could I have gotten to this point? I wondered how I would ever get back to being myself again. I didn't feel like myself, and I didn't like who I was becoming. I thought about what I had said and felt terrible about it all day. I knew that I had to make things right. I apologized to our neighbor before the sun went down.

> "'*In your anger, do not sin*': *Do not let the sun go down while you are still angry*." Ephesians 4:26 (NIV)

I'm grateful that my apology was accepted with open arms. After tears and a heartfelt discussion, I left with a feeling of freedom and a changed heart.

In the weeks that followed, I did a lot of soul searching. I knew that Jamie and I had gotten off track. It wasn't intentional. It never is, is it?

During a church sermon years ago, the preacher made a point that has always stuck with me: Sin will take you further than you want to go, keep you longer than you want to stay, and make you pay more than you intended to pay. By the world's standards, Jamie and I weren't "bad people." We were good-hearted, responsible, and willing to help others, but we were not in alignment with God. We had stopped attending church during COVID and had not found our way back. We had been hurt by some things that happened during that time. At this point, Jamie was completely against church, and I knew that finding another church home would take time. Even if he was willing, it would require planning to leave Caesar at home alone. We had tried leaving him at home alone for just a few hours, and he always found a way to get to his paw, even though we put him in a cone. It had become almost comical how he could twist and turn to show us that we weren't going to restrict him. We had begun to call him Houdini.

Once again, God's timing was evident when a friend and neighbor spoke to me about some of the wonderful teachers in the Sunday School class she and her husband attended. I knew God wanted me back in church, but trying to make this happen without getting a sitter for Caesar was going to be challenging.

We finally decided to ask my mom if she would stay with him so we could at least try the Sunday School class. Caesar loved my mom, and we had learned that if he tried to bite at his paw, the easiest (and safest) way to get him to stop was to spray him with water. He would cock his head and give you a dirty look, but he would stop and not try to bite.

So, Mom arrived on a Sunday morning to babysit her furry grandchild, and off we went, leaving her armed with a spray-bottle and doggie treats.

Attending a new church can sometimes be intimidating, but I was amazed at how welcoming and comfortable everyone made us feel. The church was large, but it never felt large. Everyone communicated, and it was evident that they worked together behind the scenes to create such an organized, loving environment.

God began to work in my heart, and his timing was and is perfect. We were starting to get settled in church when I was reminded of a business trip I had taken almost seven years ago. I was in Marshalltown, Iowa, and had gone in search of a Christian bookstore. The book I purchased on that visit was titled *A Wife's 40-day Fasting and Prayer Journal* by

Kaylene Yoder. I had bought it that day with every intention of starting it when I returned home from the trip, but God knew it would be needed for this season in my life.

I have prayed my entire life, as long as I can remember. I was raised in a Christian home and was saved when I was fourteen. However, until I read this book, I hadn't thought much about fasting. I had never felt called to fast before, but for some reason, at that time, I did. I knew that I desperately needed God back in first place in my life, and I wanted Jamie to remember that he needed Him, too.

I read the guidance at the front of the book and prepared myself for forty days of complete dedication to God. I knew that fasting in Biblical times meant completely refraining from food, but Kaylene explains that there are also other ways to practice this spiritual discipline. Her guide leads you through a different fasting choice each day, such as fasting one meal, fasting all sweets, and so on. A few days recommend no solid food, relying only on broths and juices for sustenance. Each day, the book offers a guided prayer topic for your husband, including prayer for a right heart, a right mind, self-control, obedience, and, most importantly for me, trusting God for His promises. I tend to rush things and try to get ahead of God, and every time I do, I create problems.

> *"In their hearts humans plan their course, but the Lord establishes their steps."* Proverbs 16:9 (NIV)

As I planned to move forward, I knew that I should keep this verse at the forefront of my mind. It reminded me that I was not in control. Complete reliance on God is the only way.

When I make plans without first seeking God, I can just see him shaking his head and thinking, "There she goes again."

By the end of the first week of following this devotion, I felt closer to God than I had in a long time. Whenever I began to feel hungry or craved the item that was off-limits for the day, I reminded myself of the sacrifice Jesus made for me. In addition to the book, I started studying my Bible again with a renewed heart, and it became clear that I still had some work to do. I was grieving over past events that I had not yet completely surrendered to God, and while my heart was healing from years of trials and disappointments, I still placed a barrier around it, trying not to get too close to people for fear of being hurt again.

Tenth Avenue North released a song in 2010 titled "Healing Begins." The lyrics of this song are powerful; they describe the hypothetical walls we can build around ourselves to protect our hearts.

I knew that I had built some walls, and they were centered around pride. Not temporary walls that are haphazardly constructed to withstand a small storm, but rather walls that were intended to be permanent and repel anything life threw my way. I was allowing the devil to keep me in a pit, focused on my past sins and where I had failed, rather than claiming the sanctification and restoration that God promises. I realized that I had to let go and be open to being vulnerable again to both give and receive love as God intended.

As I continued to read, study, and pray, I also began journaling my daily prayers. This practice kept me more focused and helped me get to the root of some of my thoughts.

One issue that had bothered me for years in our marriage was the lack of devotional time together. Perhaps you have experienced this too—desperately wanting your husband to be on the same page and seek God with you. I specifically desired this for the challenges our children faced during that time. In previous years, the more I asked Jamie about it, the more conflict arose between us. I couldn't understand why. My husband had been a Christian for almost thirty years. I knew he prayed daily and publicly when asked. Why was this so difficult?

One morning, while watching the sun rise during my quiet time with God, it dawned on me that I was being just as difficult as Jamie. My husband was a Christian. He was also a good provider, a loving husband, and a caring, attentive father to our kids. He had been my best friend since we were eighteen. Why in the world was I fixating on this one thing that bothered me so much? The solution was so simple that I'm embarrassed it took me so many years and so much conflict to realize it. With all the heartache we had faced, I didn't want to feel alone. While I know that God is always there, Jamie is the one person in flesh and blood who has been through the fire with me. He knew the hurt and anger I've felt and the tears I've cried, and I needed to know that he was with me, praying specifically about these things.

The next morning, I wrote five prayer requests on a sticky note and hung it on Jamie's bathroom mirror. He never said a word about it for two days! I could feel my blood pressure rising again, but I waited for a good moment, kept my voice very matter-of-fact, and said, "Did you happen to see my sticky note?" He looked at me as though I had two heads and said, "Well, of course. I've prayed about those things for the last two days." Oooooohhhhh! That man can push my buttons without doing a thing. But all kidding aside, a simple sticky note was all it took to open the door for us to begin communicating about things we needed to pray for together.

I was starting to feel the tension between Jamie and me leave our home when Caesar's health took a rapid decline. Things worsened as dementia set in with a vengeance, and we waited to see if he would snap out of it once more. This time was so much worse ... to the extent that Jamie slept with him on the living room floor for four nights. He was disoriented most of the time and bit Jamie so severely on the hand that he will probably have a scar for life. After a painful discussion with our vet and coming to terms with the fact that he no longer had a quality of life, Caesar, as they say, "crossed the rainbow bridge," passing away two days after I completed the forty days of fasting and prayer.

On the evening that Caesar passed, I arranged a conference call with the kids. Getting the four of us together while juggling work schedules and two different time zones literally requires an act of God, and God blessed us with an open window that night for which I'll be forever thankful. Jamie and I have sometimes felt that we did not fulfill our role in helping the kids develop a solid relationship with the Lord. The time from their birth until they left seems like a vapor, passing too quickly. While we can't go back, we are hopeful that they will see the difference in our lives moving forward and model the same Christian behavior for our future grandchildren. During that call we reminisced about all the good times with Caesar and how he had helped us raise them. We also discussed our renewed faith in God, assuring them that He has good things in store for them if they follow His guidance and laws in their lives. Hearing Jamie validate the changes he observed after the 40 days of fasting and prayer encouraged me further, reaffirming that God blesses obedience.

We are now completely empty-nested, and every step has been bittersweet. We have always been very close to our kids; we made them our life, and they are our greatest blessings. Kristen flew the nest in 2014, followed by Parker in 2018. As I write this, Kristen is creating a new life for herself on the East Coast, following her dreams and taking another chance on love, while Parker and our daughter-in-love, Sydney, will be moving across the country for his career in pharmacy as she completes her doctorate. Having our kids so far away has required adjustment, but my prayer is always that God will take them as far away from me as He needs to; as long as He keeps them close to Him, because before they are mine, they are His.

Life without Caesar has been another significant adjustment. He was a member of our family for fourteen years. Our children would jokingly tell you that he was our favorite child. Our parents bought him Christmas presents just as they did for their other grandchildren. All jokes aside, though, it is how we treated him ... as our third child, and this is the first time we have been completely empty-nested since our oldest was born thirty years ago.

We went through a period of grief, but as my daughter, who is wise beyond her years, likes to remind us, “Don’t cry because it's over, smile because it happened."[12] I will always smile when I think of our Caesar.

I look forward to the new life Jamie and I will build in the coming months and years. As I write this, we are getting involved at our church and will become members next month. We have made new friends and are having fun; our Life Group (which other churches call Sunday School) digs deeply into scripture, and we learn more each week. We just completed our first pickleball lesson, and what a blast that was! The mission of our church is to create disciples with hearts ablaze and pursue The Great Commission with joyful urgency, and we are so excited to be part of this! However, as we progress in life, I know that Jamie and I will also remember some lessons that the fiery little furball taught us. They are simple lessons that should be applied in our relationships as we strive to love others in the way that Jesus intends.

Next Steps

- Love unconditionally. A dog is the best reflection of Jesus that I can think of when it comes to unconditional love. They demand nothing of you other than accepting their love. They are always overjoyed to see you, even on your bad days.
- Wag your tail when you're happy—let people know that you love and appreciate them every chance you get. Life is short, so never miss this opportunity.

---

12 Attributed to Dr. Seuss.

- Be loyal – stand with your people through good times and bad.
- Enjoy the present moment—be like Caesar, live for the ride!

Chapter 10

My Nest Isn't Empty: The Lord Lives Here

By Karen Joy Cummings

FOR I KNOW THE PLANS I HAVE FOR YOU," DECLARES THE LORD, "PLANS TO PROSPER YOU AND NOT TO HARM YOU, PLANS TO GIVE YOU HOPE AND A FUTURE. JEREMIAH 29:11 (NIV)

"That was the day our lives were supposed to be normal again," someone exclaimed. In the stillness of the moment, as people turned to look toward the voice, I realized it was mine.

It was 2009. My friends and I were visiting the Flight 93 memorial in Shanksville, PA. At that time, the organic memorial to those who died on September 11, 2001, was still there. Since then, the permanent structure has been erected, trees have been planted, and bridges have been built. I visited since, but I'm not sure which memorial touched me more. Forty passengers and crew sacrificed their lives to save others. It was emotional, heart-wrenching, sad, and personal.

My empty nesting had begun the week before this tragedy. On September 2, 2001, my husband, Jerry, died from the awful disease called cancer. September 11, 2001, was the day my kids went back to school. I began to contemplate how to move forward, take care of my boys, take care of the house, and earn enough money. For 14 years, I had been a stay-at-home mom. How do we move forward with our personal loss at such a scary time for our country?

How do I survive an almost empty nest when my spouse is the first to go? How can I be both Mom and Dad when I constantly wonder if I am even a good Mom? Now I'm a single parent by no choice of my own. My youngest child is only eight. Did I make mistakes? Yeah, lots of them. Sometimes, God would tap me on the shoulder and say, "You didn't ask Me about that."

Anyone who has experienced a member of their household passing knows it takes a long while to realize they will not be walking in the door at the end of a workday. They will not be around to celebrate birthdays, holidays, and anniversaries. You still expect the daily chores they did to be done. But you also notice there is less laundry, more leftover food, and less family time as each member tries to encompass their life without their loved one.

I can also speak to being alone through divorce. When you experience a divorce, there is still a loss similar to a death. A marriage you thought would last and didn't. What about the plans you made for the future? Will you lose friends? Maybe you are moving to a new location. Are you being left alone in the family home with your memories, good and bad? I married my high school sweetheart when we were too young. I struggled to make it work. I wanted to live in a happy home, and it wasn't. After the divorce, I learned to survive with less income, which can be tough. I needed to be frugal. I was making all the decisions by myself, I was lonely, I was second-guessing *everything*, including the divorce.

Part of the reason for leaving the marriage was my upbringing in an alcoholic, co-dependent home. Although nonviolent, we were always walking around the elephant in the room. I wanted that happy home. I was the middle child, wondering where I fit in, at home and at school. In some ways, I was too independent for my own good, but still relied heavily on others' opinions. Normally able to see both sides of any issue, I was always stuck in the middle, which is why I suffered from people-pleasing, low self-esteem, insecurity, and poor decision-making skills. I thought something was wrong with me because I couldn't pick a side or make a quick decision.

In addition to that, I attended 12 years of Catholic school, learning about God, learning all the rules, especially how to fit in the boxes we were expected to live in. Although my belief in God was strong, I believed Him to be a stern judge who saw all we did wrong. No matter how good I tried to be, it would never be good enough. Which is true, but I didn't know or understand the unconditional love part back then. My faith wavered at times. Then, I heard a preacher on the radio talking about a personal relationship with God. This was a new idea for me. I kept listening & it finally sunk in. God was always with me. I began to talk to Him about everything. It became second nature. It didn't happen overnight; it won't happen overnight. I believe it is a lifelong process. A journey full of joy, comfort, compassion, and unconditional love. God was now my first love.

And then I met Jerry. He had purchased a house before we began dating with the 'home improvement' mindset that befalls many a man. This house needed a lot of work, but the price was right, and he planned to do most of the remodeling himself. To say it was a money pit was an understatement! His elderly parents lived close by and needed help, so selling and moving was not an option. When he purchased this piece of real estate, built pre-1900, there was no furnace. This house had gas-burning fireplaces in every room! During his first winter there, the water pipes froze in the bathroom and burst, leaving a gaping hole in the living room ceiling. Soon after, a new furnace was installed, and since the whole house needed to be remodeled anyway, the ductwork was easy to install up the walls that were already there! We started repairs the summer before our wedding. I wanted newer kitchen appliances and a washer and dryer in the basement, so no more going to the laundromat.

Expecting to be carried over the threshold when we arrived home the morning after our wedding, we could barely open the front door because of all the boxes I brought from my apartment. I moved into a house with crooked floors, that hole in the living room ceiling, rattly windows, a moldy bathroom, and ugly, ugly wallpaper. We were combining two households, and we had doubles of everything. Maybe that was the beginning of the over-cluttering. My boxes were stored in the attic or in the basement until I had 'time' to go through them and decide what to keep and what to donate or trash. When we first married, I still had an auditing position that required weekly travel. I was only home on the weekends and didn't want to or have time to go through old boxes. A few months later, I resigned from auditing and worked locally again. We were constantly working on the house. We wanted to start a family, and soon I was pregnant. We finished the nursery with less than a week before my first son was born! But it was finished. I have memories and pictures of the boys as toddlers with hammers breaking through the walls! We invested substantial amounts of money in this house, and it was NEVER finished! It improved, but it was not finished.

When Jerry died, there was an open wall in our bedroom that still had joists showing, needing drywall. About five years later, I purchased a few pieces of drywall and had my sons cover the hole over Christmas break. At least the joists were no longer showing. But the paste and the paint took a few years to finish. Do I procrastinate?

When my older son, Eddie, left for college, the number in our household was reduced again. Although he was home for summers, holidays, and some weekends, our household was now mostly down to two. At the end of his college years, he was offered a position in Maryland, and he accepted, and now it was permanently two: me and my younger son, Matt.

The homestead remained status quo. I did what was necessary to keep it clean, but more remodeling was out of the question. Since I had been a stay-at-home mom and I needed to build up my income. I went back to university to finish my degree in Theology and found work at a local church.

My younger son, Matthew, finished his high school years and was working odd hours and hanging out with friends, so many times I was home alone. He stayed with me for a few years, which was nice. We were both adults, so life was easy.

He moved out of the house and in with his fiancée, and they married during the COVID pandemic.

I survived; my kids survived—not through power of our own. Through it all, I prayed. I knew God was with us. At least I hoped he was. I had nothing else to hold onto.

With both of my sons married, I was an empty nester. Was the house finished? No, it was not. Did I want to finish it? No, I did not. Did I want to invest more money to complete it? No, I did not. At this point, I knew what I didn't want. But what did I want?

Overwhelmed and paralyzed. These were my biggest setbacks, and in some ways, still are. I might have some ADHD tendencies, too. I really DIDN'T know where to start. I tried so many times. What made me get serious about getting rid of the 'stuff' was trying to write. I usually sat at the dining room table with my laptop. While trying to be creative, the voices were louder than the click, click of the keyboard.

"What voices?" you ask. The voices of all the 'stuff' trapped in bags in the closets and the 'unknowns' smothering in boxes in the basement!

"Get me out of here! Help! Save me!" they cried. I knew I could not get serious writing done until I got rid of the 'stuff.'

The Holy Spirit was nudging me so I could get to those plans that God had prepared for me. I knew I needed to move forward. When I finally made the time and found the energy to 'go through' my bags, I found papers and magazines that were months old (maybe years), duplicates of the tools I could not find, and just an accumulation of junk that no one would ever need or want. Whew! I could not continue to live in this house without making some major changes.

Enter Ann, a good friend, a decorator, and an organizer. She was positive she could help me. I know God sent her to help me learn and grow. In tears, embarrassed to let her see the insides of my closets, basement, and attic, I trusted God! Her first words were, "Oh, this is so doable!" She was so encouraging. At first, when I pulled things out of bags or boxes, I felt like I had to explain to her why I kept whatever it was. She didn't want or need an explanation. She'd give me 'the look' and I would toss it in the trash. Over and over, she reminded me that I wouldn't even remember what I'd thrown away. When I hesitated over a decision, she would give me 'the look' *and* shake the garbage bag, meaning I had to trash it. She was right, after it was gone, I didn't even remember what I tossed into the trash! I was calling her my "bag shaker." I started to see hope at the end of the tunnel. The light would be brighter if I focused more time on decluttering. STUFF still claimed the rooms of the house, and no one else lived here. It was all up to me. Whether I moved or not, I had an attic and a basement that needed to be cleaned out! Turns out it took about two years!

I gave many preschool toys from the attic to a neighbor who worked with underprivileged children. I sold some things online and at a yard sale. Did I say I hate yard sales? They can sometimes be unavoidable. I took some old clothes to a vintage resale shop and came home with a few hundred dollars. Jewelry to a gold shop and made a few hundred more!

Being in my empty nest, with many of the things gone, I started to feel the dark clouds and ghosts of years past creeping into my thoughts, and they were sometimes overwhelming. "I have to get out of here!" I said to myself and anyone who would listen! Many reminders of Jerry being sick, the grief we all felt, and the nudges I felt to start a new life. After two years of sorting, trashing, and donating "stuff," I was ready to decide if I wanted to sell the house and move. I made some simple cosmetic changes to the house, like the bedroom wall that still needed paint, and put it on the market.

Being retired and in my sixties, I wanted to use my money for travel, to experience things I had always dreamed about, not fixing up an old house. I wanted to pick up the phone and call a landlord and tell him something needed fixing! Others sometimes didn't understand why I wanted to give up the security in my home, which had no mortgage, to move into an apartment where the rent would increase, my neighbors could be noisy and dirty, and my landlord could be a slum lord. But I could not continue to live in a house with so many memories.

I started looking for an apartment. The last thing I wanted was for my house to sell and have nowhere to go! I was looking online for apartments to rent when a stone house popped up on the screen in front of me. With a stone side porch! A duplex, first floor available! Wow. I fell in love with it before I even saw the inside! I called the number and did not get an answer or a voicemail. Frustrated, thinking it would be gone, I drove to the house and found a different number on a For Rent sign in the yard. I called the number, talked to the landlord, and made an appointment to see it. The inside was better than the outside. I wanted this apartment. But when would my house sell? Could I afford to pay double utilities, taxes, rent, etc.? I felt a powerful sense of the Holy Spirit telling me this was the place for me to continue my empty nesting. The front door of the apartment had a small stained-glass window with a chalice in it! How could this NOT be a sign from the Lord that I had to trust?

People said, "Your house isn't sold."

"I know," I replied.

But I knew God led me here, and it would all work out. Two months later, in April, I moved in. My house was still on the market, so I was paying rent and double utilities and taxes, which made me a little nervous. But I trusted God and knew this was His plan for me. My house finally sold in August, four months after I moved out. It was the perfect time as I was running a little low on savings. Four offers came and went. But, because of my faith and my personal relationship with God, I was able to calmly admit, "It's not my time."

This experience gave me the time and space to grow with confidence beyond my people-pleasing, low self-esteem, and insecurity. I can honestly admit that I am a better person now than I was when I moved!

What I Learned from My Hardships and Having the Courage to Embrace Empty Nesting

1) Through it all, God was with me. Through it all, I prayed. I have no clue where I'd be today if I hadn't relied on God through the difficulties of my life. God isn't out there somewhere, up in the clouds. God is right here, beside me, beside you. Here with us now. We can talk to him; listen to him—He's here to help us. It's for a lifetime! Having a personal relationship with God is the way we can get through this mess we call life and find peace, hope, joy, and love! Once

you have a personal relationship with the Trinity, you can open your mind and heart to receive God's unconditional love and blessings. You can feel the love of the Father. He made you just as He wanted and needed you to lead others to Him. He loves you with all your faults and imperfections, with all your scars, wounds, and broken pieces. Every day, thank God for loving you. Every day, you will feel His love more. Ask Jesus to be your best friend. He will give you excellent advice, suffer along with you, and hold you when you cry. The Holy Spirit brings you wisdom, which leads you to the path of blessings and love if you choose to follow it. All three love you unconditionally.

2) After you realize how much God loves you and that He doesn't make mistakes, you can begin to love and forgive yourself. It's difficult if you have lived with and still live with guilt from past sins and mistakes. Forgive yourself. Jesus already forgave you and died for your sins. Accept His forgiveness! God made us all different. We have unique gifts. Do not compare yourself to others. Don't people please. Trust your gut first. You do need to make the distinction between helping someone in real need and someone trying to manipulate you. Talk to God about it. He will give you wisdom. When I turned sixty, I was looking through photos of past years. I noticed I looked good in some of them. Yet I can still remember looking in the mirror and seeing all my flaws, thinking I was ugly. I realized this is the youngest I am ever going to be, and this is probably the best I am going to look

physically. So, I put together a photo album starting with my birth announcement up to the current time. I used them all, loving myself through my awkward preteen and teenage years. Loving myself through my sad times, finally loving myself in this stage, even with all my flaws. Don't wait as long as I did. Start loving yourself NOW. Remember, God already does. Here is a poem and some quotes I've adopted that helped me.

"There is freedom waiting for you,
On the breezes of the sky
And you ask, "What if I fall?"
Oh, my darling!
What if you fly?"

Erin Hanson[13]

"Beauty begins the moment you decide to be yourself." Coco Chanel[14]

"Blessed are the curious, for they shall have adventures." Lovelle Drachman[15]

3) Set boundaries to take care of yourself. I decided to rent this apartment completely on my own. It may have been the first decision I made without discussing with anyone. I was so excited! This was the place for me. I signed the papers. Again, I was so excited! When I finally told my family and friends, they seemed surprised that I hadn't asked for their

13 Attributed to Erin Hanson; original source unverified.

14 Attributed to Coco Chanel; original source unverified.

15 Attributed to Lovelle Drachman; original source unverified.

opinion. I knew God was in control. He had my back. And I needed to start my new life completely on my own. Set your boundaries. You don't have to say yes to everyone who makes a request. It may be a lifelong habit, but you can change it. Reply, "Let me get back to you," or "I'm not sure. I'll call you back." Then really decide if it's something you want to do. Remember, you don't owe anyone a reason for saying no. You can just say, "I am not able to do that now." You don't have to apologize. Women are often quick to apologize for everything. Most times, there is nothing to be sorry for. Sometimes, we focus more on what we can't do well instead of concentrating on our gifts and talents. Loving and giving ourselves grace. A little secret I discovered is knowing the difference between judgments and facts. For example, I am not highly organized. Am I judging myself and feeling bad about it, wondering why I'm not as organized as someone else? Or do I accept it as a fact? I don't like to cook. Fact. Sometimes I need to, and I do okay. Facts not judgements. You get the picture. You have other gifts and talents; focus on those. Offer to help in ways you can enjoy.

4) Create a bucket list if you don't already have one. What do you remember doing as a child that brought you joy? Was it drawing or coloring? Was it reading or writing? Was it building blocks or doing puzzles? Was it playing with friends or being alone? Was it cooking with grandma? Was it playing in the woods and climbing trees? Think about this and figure out what made you happy then and what will make you

happy now. Add that to your weekly or monthly list of things to do. When you no longer enjoy it, change it up. This is your time to become who God made you to be. Your empty nest is a new chapter in your book of life! When you start a new project or find a new interest, you may need to let something else go. Release the one that brings you the least joy or the one that feels most like an obligation and not a choice. Try something different frequently, follow your curiosity, not the "shoulds." Let the Holy Spirit guide you.

Conclusion

Take the next big or small step that has been weighing on your heart. Trust God to guide you to the path that is right for you. Remembering that it will happen in God's time, not in your time. I took a huge step and sold my house to move into an apartment. Four offers came and went. Because of my faith, I was able to calmly admit, "It's not my time," even though money was dwindling. I love living on my own. I have a lovely apartment, good friends, and time for prayer and God. I eat cereal for dinner when I want, and write when I'm on a roll. Some days I sleep in until 10:00 am or later. I am retired, working one day a week, whatever time and day I choose. Life is good. So is empty-nesting! But my nest isn't empty; God is always here. And God is always with me. Today, right now, I accept His unconditional love and forgiveness.

Suggestions for Next Steps

Are you familiar with KLove radio or the KLove app? It's all Christian music, 24/7. The DJs encourage a 30-day challenge. Listen to nothing but Christian music for 30 days and see if it doesn't change your life, your attitude. I have listened to KLove radio since they came to my town in September 2009. So many wonderful songs to lift your day and mood and bring you closer to God. I know most of the lyrics and sing in my car or in my empty nest. Another reason to love your nest. You can sing and dance whenever you please! Look for Christian websites to follow or podcasts to listen to. I downloaded the Hallow app (https://hallow.com/). This is a Catholic site and has many different passages to listen to, Scripture, devotionals, and prayers. Give one of them a try.

Join a faith community if you don't already have one. It's okay to take baby steps or even check out a few to decide where you belong. Small groups are a positive way to meet people and learn from each other about Scripture, prayer, or even support for your empty nest life. Take a walk in your neighborhood several times a week. Talk to your neighbors, get to know them. Soon you will be sharing their porches or patios and a sweet tea!

Start a gratitude or daily journal. Any notebook will do, or even your computer. However, I love the feeling of a pen in my hand and writing or drawing pictures. And I must admit, one of my passions is buying pretty notebooks! I have more than I need, but still cannot pass up buying another charming one! Write your thoughts, good and bad. I have found that sometimes I get answers while I am writing. Even on your bad days, you will be able to find something to be grateful for. Look for the miracles in everyday life. God loves you!

About the Authors

*

Karen Griffith

Karen has been blogging and writing *a little dose of divine lefse*, a weekly newsletter, since 2020. She's been an interior designer, kitchen designer, and closet designer, and is perpetually halfway through an MA in a writing program. Her background in design and love for writing came together in the later years of motherhood, and she has discovered that creating and sharing beauty, grace, and order is what home is all about, no matter what stage of life you are in! Married for 21 years, she has 2 college-aged daughters. She lives in Farmington, MN.

Connect with Karen:

Divinelefse.com

Facebook: https://www.facebook.com/divinelefse/

Instagram: instagram.com/divinelefse

Brenda Woomer

Brenda Woomer resides in southern Ohio, where she finds peace and inspiration in her garden, convinced that whispers from God are loudest amidst the dirt, blooms, and harvest. Passionate about God's word, she is dedicated to encouraging others to discover the truth of hope found within the pages of scripture. She delights in being surrounded by family and friends, whether sharing deep conversation or loud laughter. She is the mother of Seth and Jesse, grateful for over 30 years of marriage to Tom, and excited about her recent status upgrade to grandma.

Connect with Brenda:

Facebook: https://www.facebook.com/bena.sue.5
Instagram: https://www.instagram.com/bena.sue/

Jane Harper DeLong

Jane DeLong founded Pleasing Aroma Ministries to provide women with teaching and resources to deepen their walk with God. A lifetime Bible nerd, Jane's passion is helping women cultivate friendship with God through daily interaction with His Word; reading, studying, and praying the Scripture. Jane is a firm believer that every Christian should know God's Word for themselves in order to grow spiritually and keep from being deceived by the enemy. She leads moms of all ages in life-changing Bible study each week in the Raising Kids on Your Knees Zoom Room. Jane and her husband live in rural Georgia. They've been married 38 years. Together they have raised five kids and are currently enjoying the fruit of that labor by spoiling their grandkids!

Connect with Jane:

To join the Raising Kids on Your Knees Zoom Room email janedelong.pam@gmail.com

Facebook: https://www.facebook.com/jane.delong.92

Instagram: https://www.instagram.com/janehdelong/

Kathleen A. Giles

Kathleen Giles writes to encourage matriarch mamas to be spiritual influencers in their extended families. By day, she works as a church admin and is known as a communicator, Bible study teacher, bookkeeper, office manager, and the only staff member who can unjam the copier. She loves being in community with other writers and enjoys editing and giving feedback. Kathleen and her husband live in upstate NY but escape to Alaska whenever possible. They are blessed with two happily married children who live locally. Kathleen funds her writing life through custom sewing and alterations.

Connect with Kathleen:

https://kathygiles.com/

Instagram: https://www.instagram.com/kgiles87/

Hope Intercedes

Hope Intercedes is in a continual state of learning how to depend on God through prayer. She loves collecting scripture passages to put in her prayer books. Laying a foundation for HOPE and building on the certainty and expectancy of God's character and promises. You can find her at a nearby park strolling hand in hand with her husband as they walk by faith united in prayer. She also enjoys playing board games, baking, reading, sewing, organizing *anything*, and LAUGHTER!

Amy Duckworth Harrington

Amy is a wife and mother of two college aged boys living in Central Pennsylvania. She has been busy writing many words while listening to country music. She enjoys taking photos of the green light within the ocean waves and recreating them on canvas. She has fun hitting all types of balls; golf, pickle and tennis balls inside or outside. Amy loves to tromp through the woods, garden in the yard, walk the beach, collect shells, identify new birds and protect the plovers on the shorelines. She is happiest with her family sitting together, playing games and reading by a roaring fire. She is always *ready for* the next adventure.

Connect with Amy:

www.amyduckworthwrites.com

Facebook: https://www.facebook.com/profile.php?id=100008849317351

Instagram: https://www.instagram.com/amyduckworth13/

LinkedIn: https://www.linkedin.com/in/amy-d-0267601a4/

Francesca Follone-Montgomery, OFS

Francesca Follone-Montgomery (MA, MSW) is an Italian American secular Franciscan (OFS) from Firenze, Italy, who seeks God in others, all aspects of life, and creation. She moved to America desiring to sing Jazz, yet God had other plans: Being a wife, a mother, a Catholic bookstore employee, an office manager at NRLC, an Italian university teacher, a life coach, and a published author. She desires to communicate God's love to all, encouraging them to joyfully embrace the plans God has for every one of His children. Francesca has also published four children's stories: *The Journey, The Friend, The Plan, and The Song.*

Connect with Francesca:

www.smileandsootheyourself.com

LinkedIn: https://www.linkedin.com/in/francesca-fol-lone-montgomery-bba1b07a/

Michelle Castro-Proud

Michelle is a mother and "Mimi" from Southern California, She has worked in accounting for more than 35 years but has always enjoyed casual, personal writing that has allowed her to place her most treasured moments, thoughts, and ideas on paper. This is her first opportunity to write her story for others to read. Her prayer is that others may relate to her story of love and separation. In addition to traveling to the northern part of the state to see her three adorable grandsons about once a month, she also loves to spend time with family and friends.

Connect with Michelle:

Instagram: https://www.instagram.com/mproud66/
Facebook: https://www.facebook.com/michelle.proud.7

Melissa Lindsey

Melissa believes God does not call the equipped; he equips the called. The only requirements are to be willing and ready. She is a data analyst who works in bank conversions and has more than twenty years of experience in the banking industry. She currently lives in Western Kentucky with her husband. They have two grown children and one daughter-in-law. She loves bookstores, the ocean, and a great cup of coffee.

Connect with Melissa:

www.therippling brook.com
Email: theripplingbrook@gmail.com

Karen Joy Cummings

Karen Joy Cummings, writes for sensitive, insecure women to overcome perfectionism and people pleasing from past trauma, to set boundaries and become the woman of joy and blessing that God created her to be. A widow for over twenty years and the mother of two married sons, she loves being a storyteller. She authored a piece in "Clunk on the Head, How the Holy Spirit Got Our Attention," by Gina Napoli. She graduated from Carlow University with a BA in Theology at the age of fifty-five, where she received an award for Excellence in Ministry. She is a retired ministry worker living in Pittsburgh PA.

Connect with Karen:

www. karenjoycummings.com

Facebook: https://www.facebook.com/karenjoy.cummings.7

Instagram: https://www.instagram.com/KarenJoyCummings

Closing

Dear Reader,

Thank you for reading *Reclaiming Me: Embracing Life and Purpose with an Empty Nest*!

I want to take a moment to celebrate the incredible authors who contributed to this meaningful book. They have poured their hearts into discovering, clarifying, and sharing their unique messages—and now, you get to benefit from their hard work and dedication.

At hope*books, we are deeply proud of our authors and are honored to partner with them on this journey. If you've ever considered writing and publishing your book, we invite you to visit hopebooks.com to learn more about our coaching and publishing services. We believe that everyone has a message to share and an audience to serve, and the world needs your hopeful words now more than ever.

Once again, let's take a moment to celebrate the hard work of these authors in bringing *Reclaiming Me* to life.

Sincerely,

Brian Dixon

Publisher, hope*books

Made in the USA
Columbia, SC
17 June 2025

94927310-b6c4-4a77-8032-68f06e802a8cR01